Y0-CFR-351

GUY CODE

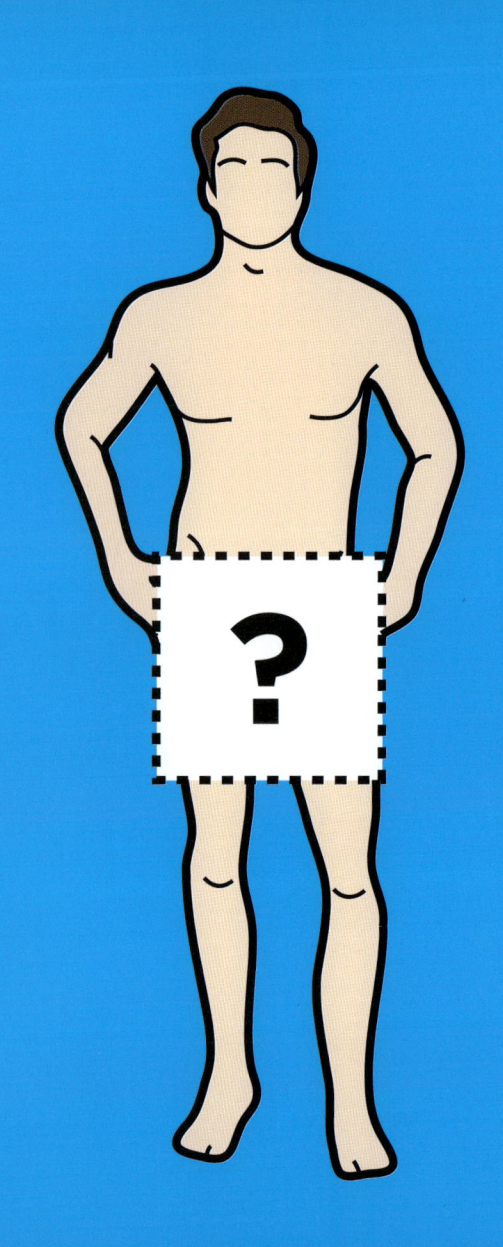

UNLEASH YOUR MANHOOD

BY NOAH LEVENSON

TABLE OF CONTENTS

CHAPTER	PAGE
INTRODUCTION	5
MANSCAPING	8
BATHROOM PRODUCTS	18
HAVING A FRIEND IN TOWN	26
CRYING	36
SOCIAL NETWORKING	46
BBQS	56
BATHROOM ETIQUETTE	62
CONTRACEPTION	72
FIGHTING	80
SEXTING	88
LYING	98
DRINK LIKE A MAN	106
THE MORNING AFTER	116
THE FRIEND ZONE	126
REJECTION	132

INTRODUCTION

I am the happiest, wealthiest, most wildly successful, most desired-by-women person I know.

And it's all because of one thing:

I know *The Code*.

But with great knowledge comes great responsibility. My belief in *Guy Code* often piques the curiosity of those that I meet, and thus, everyday situations such as grocery shopping and pumping gas quickly turn to impassioned theoretical debates—once I inform whoever's behind the register that *The Code* is within them (in a hoarse whisper, while maintaining deep, scary eye contact). "Where did you learn of this?" They ask. "Who else has applied its power?" And, most frequently: "Is that debit or credit?"

Though possessing of the golden secret to eternal happiness, I try to keep stuff low-key. I am merely a humble ambassador sent forth on a crusade by the universal nation of masculinity. No big deal, really. I answer these questions patiently, illustrating the empowering effects of spiritual wealth with my AmEx Black Card. Yes—I'm very fortunate. But it wasn't always this way.

Two years ago, my life had collapsed all around me. I was a broken, hopeless, desperate shell of a person, and the suffocating walls of my own self-destruction seemed only to close tighter each day.

You see, I'd accidentally received a really cute pedicure. That was the beginning. Before I knew it, I'd begun using something I'd only seen in the movies: a loofah. *Yes*—one of those fluffy-scrubber shower things. My body wash of choice was *cinnaberry*, which is a devastating thrill-ride of cinnamon and berries. I couldn't get enough. One day I drank a Cosmopolitan—and *liked* it. Everything had spiraled out of control. Before long, my girlfriend left me for the pizza delivery guy. Then her sister left me, too. (Also for the pizza delivery guy.) I'd reached rock bottom. And it'd all happened so quickly—in thirty minutes or less. Needless to say, I paid for that pie. Dearly.

But little did I know that from my lowest moment of desperation would emerge the most powerful of personal victories.

For in those pepperonis I would discover the most delicious of truths. Two slices deep, I was suddenly possessed by a force much greater than myself. I felt as though my spirit had exited my body. And there, in the living room, I was entranced by a vision—appearing as a spectacular, magically glowing projection in the corner.

Turns out it was the TV, and my spirit just got up to grab a beer.

But it was then that I knew I'd been given the greatest gift of all. I had discovered *Guy Code*.

I'd achieved a glimpse of something more powerful than a thousand suns. It was as if light had shined upon me for the first time, and I had awoken, inexplicably, without a hangover.

Guy Code, in layman's terms, is a perpetually limitless and infinite source of positively charged kinetic spiritual energy. Basic stuff. No big deal.

The Code has no shape or form. It is not a physical object. One cannot see it or touch it. Rather, *Guy Code* is the *guiding force* that is in *all* of us. It is a set of unspoken commandments—a rulebook for existence. It is our candle in the dark—the illuminator of our path. When we need it the most, *The Code* shows us what to do—and how to do it.

And by applying its power, any man can live the life of his dreams!

My mind was pretty blown, but I needed to know more. Who else had understood this? Had *The Code* existed since the beginning of time? Was there any scientific explanation for its manifest miracles? I embarked on a journey of exploration and research. I sold the entirety of my possessions and vowed to scour the Earth for the truth. I went to New Jersey. I pored over the ancient texts of Wikipedia and Gizmodo.

Through my study, I discovered things that boggled the mind. I also learned how to play Boggle. (Don't waste your time.) As I traced the history of *The Code*, I was shocked to learn of all the people who had known it and successfully harnessed its power. These were the greatest men in history: Aristotle, Shakespeare, Einstein, Canseco.

Guy Code has been recognized for thousands of years. Behind every heroic genius was a supreme force guiding their decisions—and also at least one raspberry flirtini, drank when they thought no one was looking.

But intriguingly, the incredible results of *The Code* were not limited to great thinkers and steroid users. I discovered that millions of average (and some pretty subaverage) guys had applied it to their lives—reaping its benefits at the office, in their homes, and at the urinal.

Stunned, I asked: "Why doesn't *everybody* know this? Why isn't *Guy Code* taught in school?" I felt a burning desire to share my knowledge with the Universe. Another part of me was sorta burning too, but that's another story.

I compiled all of my research into what you now hold in your hands. In this book, you will find stunning information in support of *The Code*. You will read incredible-but-true testimonials of positivity and change from regular guys just like you. You will be asked to take a searching and fearless inventory of your inner self with multiple-choice *Code Quizzes*. You will encounter scientists, academics and learned men from every field, presenting indisputable, empirical proof of *The Code*'s worldly influence. You will discover powerful techniques—the *Mantras of Manhood*—for tuning your thoughts to the frequency of *Guy Code*.

And lastly, you will learn how *The Code* changed my life. Which, as I mentioned earlier, is pretty freaking awesome now.

It's with great pride that I present to you *Guy Code: Unleash Your Manhood*. Through its study, you will discover an infinity of information. Some of this you may have already known. Some of it will come as a surprise. And some of it you knew was coming, but the polite thing is to do is act like you didn't.

Guy Code has many times been compared to an incredible road map. Once you open it, forget about it. You'll never get this thing folded back up.

Do you know *The Code*?

CHAPTER 1
MANSCAPING

Much like the Universe itself, the *Guy Code* to Manscaping seems complex—but it actually couldn't be simpler. Some girls like men with a lot of body hair. Some girls like men with no body hair. Some girls like girls. And all men like girls who like girls.

—SCHMEPHEN SCHMAWKING

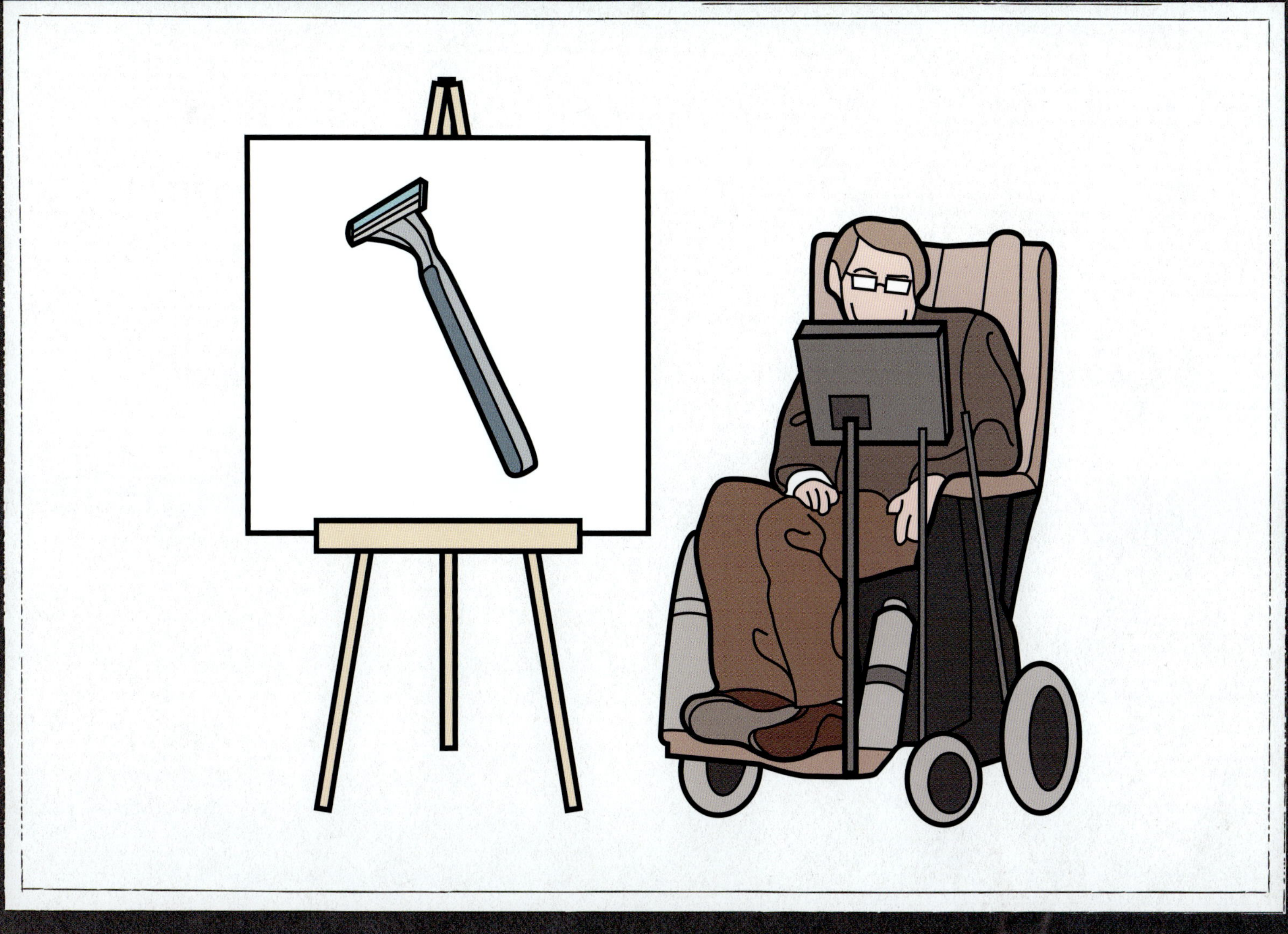

Body hair often takes us by surprise. One moment we're children, smooth and unspoiled as porcelain dolls—and the next, we overhear an embittered co-worker describing us as "hirsute." It's especially surprising if you don't know what that word means. I'll save you the trouble: it means hairy. And yes—I *am*. *Everywhere*. My arms are hairy. My hands are hairy. My neck is like a Barrel Cactus. And don't get me started on my back. I'm one of those people who said, "Back hair will never happen to me." I thought that back hair was only something you read about, until I realized that nobody's ever written about back hair. The truth is, back hair happens when you least expect it. You don't see it coming. (Because it's behind you. On your back.)

I've spent the latter half of my life wondering how all this hair got here—and what, if anything, I should do with it, how I might style it, and who to ask for a recommendation about conditioner. The first half of my life I just spent hoping it would start growing already. Be careful what you wish for.

To groom or not to groom? This, my friends, is quite a tangled question. Luckily there is one tool that can cut, shear, and snip straight to the truth: the *Guy Code* to Manscaping.

"Manscaping" itself is a wonderful word, having combined the best parts of "landscaping" with *all* the parts of "man." But what *is* manscaping? Simply put, it is the art and science of maintaining the shape, depth and thickness of the hair that grows everywhere *but* your head.

You might be asking: Is there any reason to manscape besides getting girls? There's a very simple answer: No. Trimming your pubes may make your penis look bigger, but this is not something that will interest and impress your bros. If it does, it's clear they haven't discovered *The Code*.

Through painstaking research, I've discovered that talking about body hair is not always polite dinner table conversation. And without the guidance of my peers, I remained for a long time in a state of anxiety and confusion. *Should I shave it? Or maybe just trim? What exactly is a "Brazilian," and would my dick look cool at Carnaval?* Coming to terms with my predicament, I spent many sleepless nights pondering the best approach, and also whether my health insurance covered electrolysis.

With no one to turn to, I developed a lot of primitive fears about body grooming. I believed that life held but two options for me: be mistaken for a gorilla at the beach, or submit to the nuclear radiation-burn of testicle waxing. I lived in a constant mode of suffering and panic—and after a couple of particularly frightening episodes, I switched permanently to button-fly jeans. It was only when I discovered the *Guy Code* to Manscaping that my life began to turn around.

THE TWO KINDS OF ACCEPTABLE BACK HAIR

GORILLAS

WEREWOLVES

MANSCAPING MATRIX OF STYLES

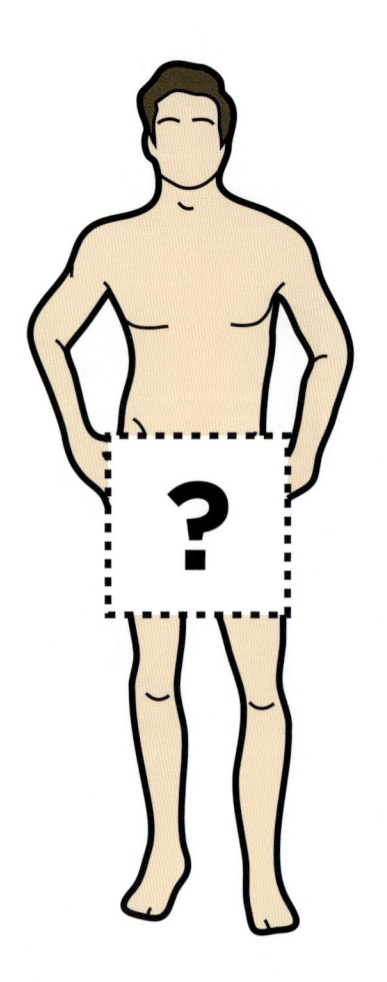

THE FIRESTARTER	THE GENE SHALIT
THE RODMAN	THE GORDON GEKKO
THE CAESAR	THE IVAN DRAGO
THE PRIVATE PYLE	THE BREAKING BAD

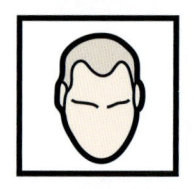

"Before I knew *The Code*, my life was all out of whack. I was working at Pottery Barn, eating chicken McNuggets every night, watching Kojak reruns until dawn. I had no idea that just one thing was standing in the way of my dreams: I was shaving my nuts bald. Who told me to do that? Nobody, that's who. I just started doing it, thinking it was cool. Turns out bald testicles aren't "cool"–but they are pretty cold. *Guy Code* taught me to look inside myself for the truth, and to look at my nuts less like Telly Savalas. I decided to let 'em grow out. Now I live in a four-and-a-half million-dollar mansion, and drive two Ferraris to the 7-11. Who loves ya, baby?"
~ Robert S., multimillionaire, former Pottery Barn employee,
    fan of Kojak

Robert's story is especially inspirational because it reveals a common mistake made by people who have yet to be enlightened: if we spend too much time thinking about what we want our genitals to look like, we will fail to consider what other people want our genitals to look like.

I THINK WOMEN THESE DAYS WANT YOU TO BE LIKE MICHAEL PHELPS: CLEAN SHAVEN, AND A HEAVY POT SMOKER. *~ Jordan Carlos*

THE SHORTER THE GRASS, THE TALLER THE TREE. YOU WANT TO MAKE SURE YOU PROTECT THAT WOOD.
~ Donnell Rawlings

CODE QUIZ

HERE'S A QUICK *CODE QUIZ* THAT WILL HELP YOU DISCOVER THINGS ABOUT YOURSELF THAT, TO BE HONEST, EVERYBODY ELSE ALREADY KNOWS, AND THEY'RE TALKING ABOUT BEHIND YOUR (HAIRY) BACK ANYWAY:

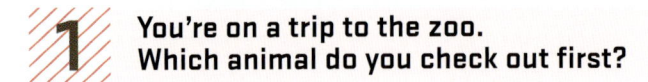

1 You're on a trip to the zoo. Which animal do you check out first?

- A BEAR
- B SNAKE
- C CHICKEN

2 Which of these phenomena do you believe is *most* likely to exist?

- A THE BERMUDA TRIANGLE
- B SASQUATCH
- C CRYSTAL PEPSI

3 Of these American presidents, which one had the best throat?

- A ABRAHAM LINCOLN
- B RICHARD NIXON
- C BILL CLINTON

4 Eating at a restaurant, you discover a hair in your Coke. Do you:

- A SEND IT BACK IMMEDIATELY
- B DRINK IT ANYWAY
- C BECOME A SUPREME COURT JUSTICE

1 ANSWER

A You may need a trim.

B You should let it grow out.

C You're not at the zoo. Who gave you those directions?

2 ANSWER

A Maybe you should send your neck hair there.

B Hairiest guy on earth— Yeti doesn't care!

C You got evidence to support this?

3 ANSWER

A You appreciate the refined nobility of a beard.

B You salute the heroic actions of a whistleblower.

C You like BJs.

4 ANSWER

A You are cautious and conservative.

B You are a risk-taker; a daredevil.

C You are Clarence Thomas.

There is no one ideal shape into which to sculpt your pubes, we must all find our perfect trim—but avoid stars, polka dots and/or hearts. This is your groin we're talking about, not your chemistry teacher's necktie. A gentle rule of thumb: You are a man, not a topiary. In certain circumstances, however, your jersey number might be kinda cool.

The Code is already within *you*. You need only accept its gift to access and unleash your full potential. Think of it like this: similar to water rushing downstream, you are already an incredible force of nature. Long ago, man recognized the power of rivers, and harnessed it with hydroelectric power plants. The electricity created is energy that begins as gravity applied to water, which is translated and converted by turbines, and flows eventually into the beard trimmer you'll use on your balls. That's pretty much basically it.

Some men are born as heir to the kingdom. You are *hair* to the kingdom. Success in body grooming is your birthright, and no one can usurp the throne. In your palace, the carpet may or may not match the drapes. It's up to you. Use the power of *Guy Code* to live up to your fullest, most luxurious potential. Or possibly a shorter/neater potential. (To make it look bigger, or whatever.) Now you know *The Code*. Live the dream.

THE CODE CONDENSED

▨ THE FIRST RULE OF MANSCAPING IS: YOU DO NOT TALK ABOUT MANSCAPING.

▨ CONTRARY TO POPULAR BELIEF, DICK HAIR DOES NOT AID IN DIGESTION. DON'T BRING IT UP AT DINNER.

▨ NO NOVELTY SHAPES.

▨ THE BEST WAY TO MAKE YOUR PENIS LOOK BIGGER IS LOCATED IN YOUR BATHROOM, NOT IN THOSE LINKS YOU KEEP CLICKING.

CHAPTER 2

BATHROOM PRODUCTS

Only loofah I want in my house is Loofah Vandross.
—DONNELL RAWLINGS

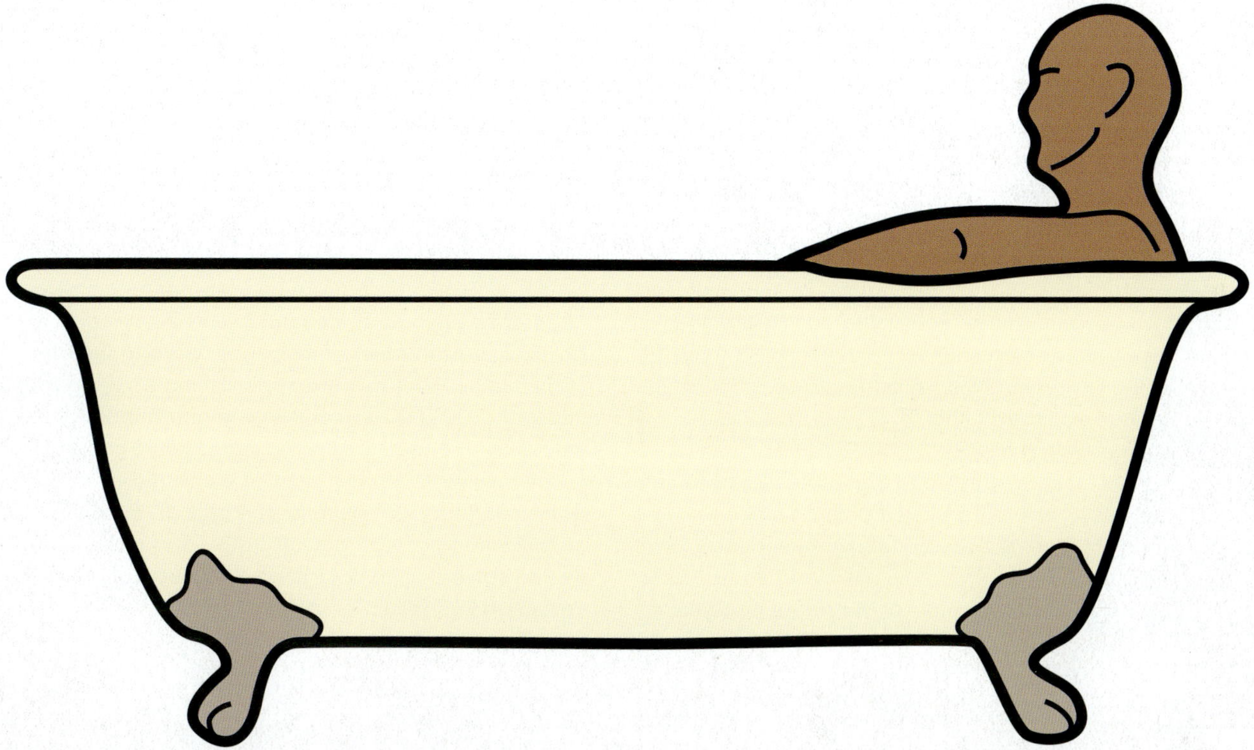

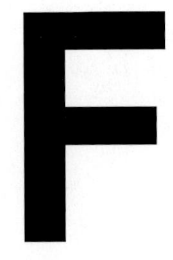

For men, bathroom products are the source of much agony—and I'm not just talking about getting some Dr. Bronner's up your you-know-what. There comes a time in every man's life when he must confront the contents of his medicine cabinet, and decide for himself which of those bottles and jars will remain on the shelf—and which of them will be opened, sniffed, and slathered liberally all over his body. Unfortunately, the correct course of action can be considerably obscure. How long to groom? Which products to use? How much to apply—and does a real man ever "lather"?

Like you, I was on a quest for knowledge—and those lotions and creams *really* freaked me out. Well, before I discovered *Guy Code*, I was lost and aimless—and I thought I could handle certain problems on *my own*.

I want to tell you about a disastrous example of just such a mistake.

Rather than seeking the power of *The Code*, I simply reversed my anxiety. I forced myself to believe that I had no problems at all. Instead of writhing tortuously with panic at the drug store, I just began to imagine that the filth and grime that accumulated on my body was *actually* a sparkling sheen of health and cleanliness. I *really* let myself go. I would jar awake each morning from the repulsive stench of my own underarms, stretch my limbs wide and say, "I feel fresh! I am splendid! My body is a bouquet of hibiscus." I'd wring the grease from my hair and imagine that I was actually brushing a luxurious and elegant coif, inhaling deeply the mineral aroma of a babbling mountain brook. "I am clean!" I'd say. "I am fresh-cut grass; I am citrus scrubbed with rose. I am a new man!" As my beard grew tangled and matted and flecked with Kraft Singles, I concentrated only on the essence of pure spring air that surely wafted from my crotch. My feeling of sweet invigoration was so powerful and energizing that it brought a tear to my eye, and I considered yodeling.

**KEEP YOUR FRIENDS CLOSE,
YOUR ENEMIES CLOSER**

AND YOUR DEODORANT CLOSEST

TOTAL TIME INSIDE THE BATHROOM, WITHOUT MASTURBATING: SEVEN AND A HALF MINUTES. *~ Donnell Rawlings*

I refused to apply even one dab of soap or swipe of deodorant, because, like I said, I was *pretty* sure I was the cleanest guy around. If my feeling of purity subsided—and I could actually make out through the eye crust the layer of slime that coated my skin, or smell the distinct odor of baked garbage that emanated from my every pore—I would suddenly feel very hopeless and sad, and also usually throw up a little into my mouth. I knew I wanted to erase that feeling, and replace it completely with the happy, free one, that was still paying for yodeling lessons. Well—as it turns out, you can't really Jedi-Mind-Trick the cheese outta your beard. My body was so hazardous, they declared my shower a Superfund site. I took off my shoes and they mobilized FEMA.

IF YOU DON'T WIPE YOUR ASS, YOU'RE GONNA DATE GIRLS THAT LOOK LIKE THEY DON'T WIPE THEIR ASS. *~ Donnell Rawlings*

We all need help sometimes. And for me, some face wash, toothpaste, and a Mach3 would've been a good place to start. Now I know: when it comes to bathroom products, only *Guy Code* can show you what to use—and *where to use it*.

HER BATHROOM ESSENTIALS

HIS BATHROOM ESSENTIALS

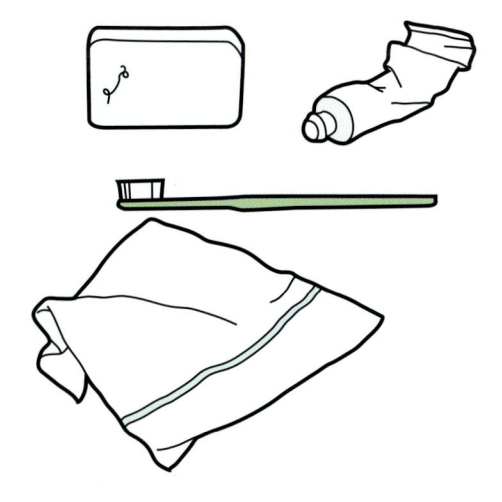

Obsessively meditating on our most terrorizing fears rarely yields a positive result. But conversely, blindly *avoiding* the harsh realities of life can result in stink lines on your graduation photo. Luckily, adjusting our negative behavior is merely a matter of inverting our reckless thoughts. *The Code*, much like Kim Kardashian, has never said "no." Practice your positivity with these *Mantras of Manhood*:

WRONG: I am completely unafraid to offend people with my body odor.
RIGHT: *I'm trying to make friends, here. Would it kill me to spritz a little Right Guard?*

WRONG: My hair looks like it came outta the janitor's closet. Hooray!
RIGHT: *Shampoo, a hat, or both?*

WRONG: I am thrilled to experiment with all the tools of the bathroom, and also my girlfriend's bathroom.
RIGHT: *A man must possess three things: soap, a clean razor, and some self-respect. Take it easy.*

WRONG: I really want to use conditioner.
RIGHT: *Fine. But stay away from the shower cap.*

WRONG: No man can judge the way I use the bathroom.
RIGHT: *They will judge the way you use the bathroom. Hurry up. And leave your phone out here.*

The bathroom is a labyrinth of complexities, and around every bend lurks a new and dangerous confrontation. You may survive your bout with thickening shampoo, but will the SPF moisturizer get the best of you? Will hair putty be your demise? These products have the power to strip a man of his decency, and also his essential oils, according to some dermatologists. But make no mistake: The most potent product of all is your *mind*. You must consider the bathroom a *pit stop* during the Indy 500 of life. You're in, you're out, change a tire, drink some Gatorade. That's it. We are racing towards the finish line! That means *no baths*.

A MAN CAN TAKE A BATH. IF HE'S SIX YEARS OLD.
~ Jordan Carlos

Ultimately, we've learned that the *Guy Code* to Bathroom Products is a matter of balance: too little attention paid, and you're living in a trash can—but *too much* attention paid and you're living like Richard Simmons. His hair doesn't get like that by accident, you know.

IF YOUR FACE WASH HAS A FACE WASH, THEN YOU'RE BREAKING GUY CODE. *~ Vinny Guadagnino*

JUMBLE

BATHROOM PRODUCTS:
Unscramble these phrases. (And if you find any of these in your bathroom, you've broken *Guy Code*.)

1. HA FOOL
2. TUBBY DOTER
3. HMM IT BIT TANK
4. WEDDING STUPOR
5. PRACTICAL RUB FIASCO
6. TRY AIR MR VINO
7. UNICORN GIRL

ANSWERS: 1. LOOFAH 2. BODY BUTTER 3. MINK BATH MITT 4. DUSTING POWDER 5. APRICOT FACIAL SCRUB 6. VANITY MIRROR 7. CURLING IRON

THE CODE CONDENSED

- YOU DO STINK.

- FILTH ATTRACTS FILTH. SEXUALLY SPEAKING.

- SHIT, SHOWER, SHAVE: IF IT AIN'T FOR ONE OF THOSE, IT AIN'T FOR ANY BROS.

- BUT WHAT HAPPENED IN YOUR GIRLFRIEND'S BATHROOM NEVER HAPPENED.

CHAPTER 3

HAVING A FRIEND IN TOWN

SIR CHARLES BEDSWERVER, DISTINGUISHED MAN OF LETTERS:
The motif of the unexpected houseguest was ubiquitous in 19th century literature. As authors increasingly chose to chronicle the details of everyday life, the often complicated plots of their novels invariably included a sudden encounter with a long-lost acquaintance, pounding upon their door in the middle of the night. Usually, this acquaintance would arrive bearing only a burlap sack—this being the implement that would best accumulate *the dust*—which, in those days, it seems, was the only thing more ubiquitous than houseguests. The novelist Flaubert himself—undoubtedly a man versed in the more esoteric of vacuum cleaner attachments—once quipped: "Shoes on the couch? Be my fucking *guest!*" It is now believed that his sarcasm was lost in translation.

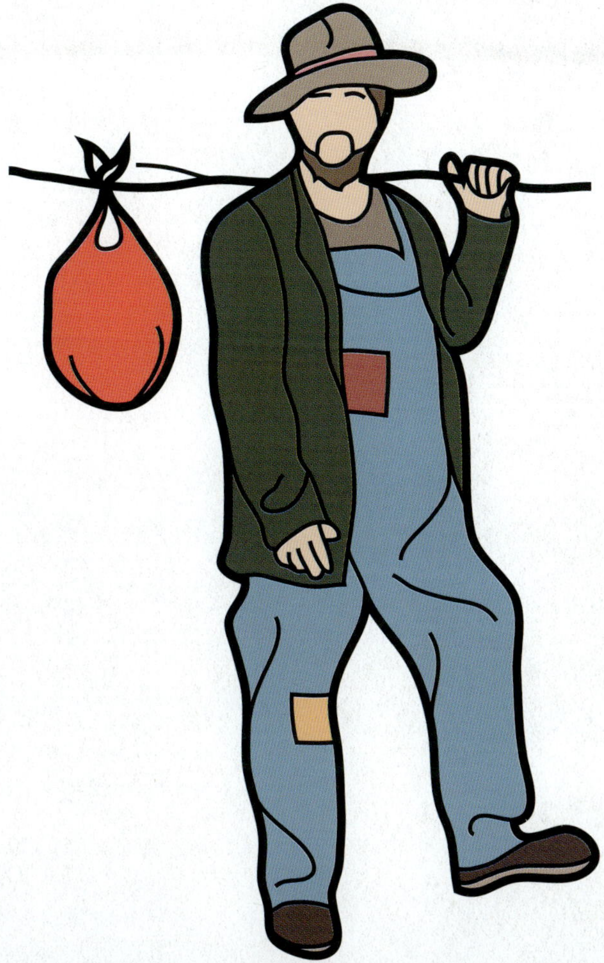

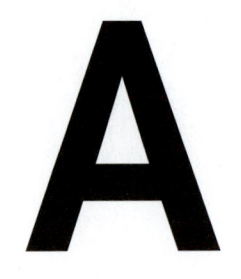

Amongst men, there is a rich and ancient tradition of hospitality. He who can provide services and amenities is often called upon, in time of need, to accommodate his fellow countrymen. I am no exception to this rule. And so, if I might humbly approach your table, *Monsieur*, I feel it's appropriate to offer a recommendation: if what you're having is *a friend in town*, the most delightful pairing might be a motel room.

Inviting a friend to crash is like ordering the pastrami Reuben: few would argue that it sounded great—but about halfway through, something's beginning to tell you this wasn't such a good idea. Day three with a houseguest is similar to that sudden alarm for which you quickly excuse yourself from the table—except you are in your own home, with no known avenue of escape—and it's some other dude unleashing large-scale depravities upon your lavatory.

Indeed—the contamination of your apartment with a Chernobyl-level shit is grounds for a revocation of operating license, if not a mandatory evacuation within a fifty-mile radius and the erection of a concrete sarcophagus over the commode. Your *bruh* from college just created an environmental "exclusion zone"—and, though the untimely death of your geraniums, Boston fern and goldfish was devastating, the final victim of this disaster will ultimately be your friendship.

WHEN YOU'RE A GUEST IN SOMEONE ELSE'S HOUSE, YOU GOTTA TREAT IT LIKE YOU'RE HIKING IN AN ENDANGERED LANDSCAPE. YOU DO NOT LEAVE BEHIND ANY TRACE OF YOURSELF. *~ Jon Gabrus*

THE FIRST SIX TO TWELVE HOURS IS AMAZING. AND AFTER THAT, YOU JUST GOT A DUDE SLEEPING ON YOUR COUCH.

~ Damien Lemon

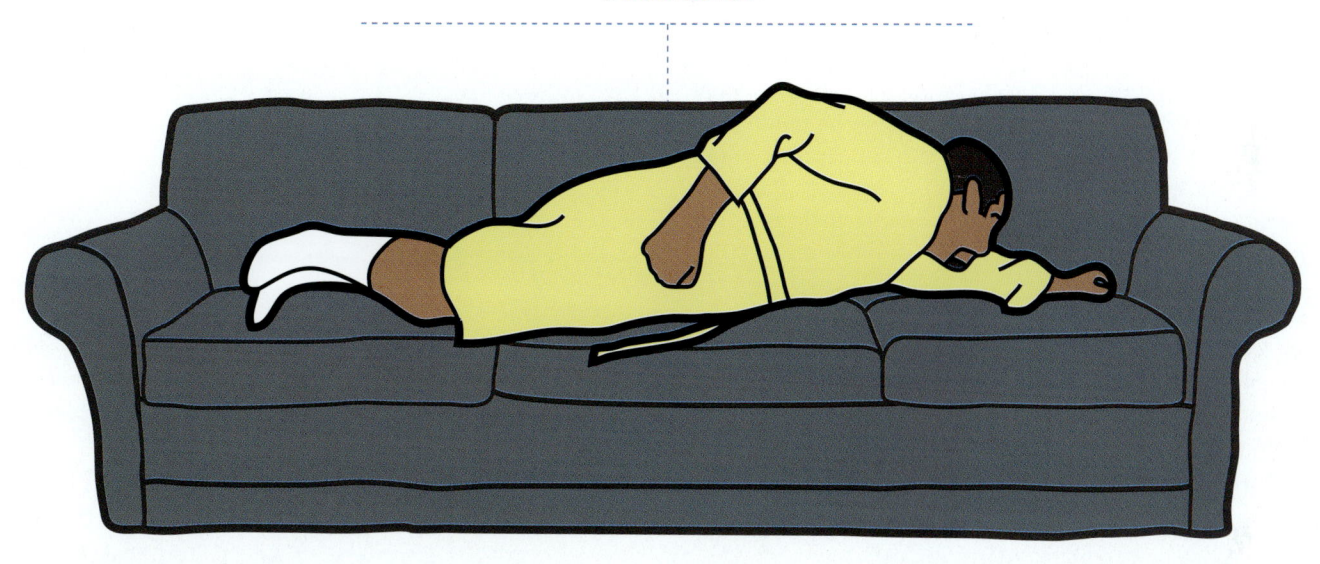

As we grow older, life takes us in many wondrous directions. For my friend-since-the-third-grade, Tommy Grasso, that direction was Karlstad, Minnesota, where he works as an envelope stuffer for a life insurance company—though he prefers the term "mail specialist." Once a year he returns East—and, each time the leaves begin to mottle and fall, and the first hint of autumn chills the air, I excitedly anticipate that great season of adhesive conferences, and my old buddy's knock upon my door.

But by day two, I'm ready to put him in the figure-four leg-lock and suplex his ass through the coffee table. Not only does he turn my living room into Fallujah, but the guy doesn't shut up about postage. You wouldn't believe how much he has to say about it. Fortunately, *The Code* has enlightened me to the most trusted method for tactfully returning unwanted *males* to sender: make your house as crappy as possible.

DR. BRADLEY SORNER, behavioral psychologist:
The so-called 'comfort zone' is a state of zero-risk—one in which a person operates only within the boundaries of certainty. If you have cable, air conditioning, Xbox Live and an unopened box of Cheez-Its, it is also your apartment—and chances are, dude's gonna be operating within its boundaries for-friggin'-ever

Though you may not consider it as such, your home is the most luxurious hotel in the neighborhood. No credit card is required for security—no one keeps tabs on the minibar—and there's no awkward bill for the pornography. Only in the hotel of your home—the *home-tel*, if you will—does the "adult movie service" flow so freely! For that reason alone, your guest will most certainly choose to extend his stay. The result? You've got a guy watching porn on your ottoman. And for *that* reason alone, an intervention is required.

SCARCITY DETERMINES VALUE

STOCK UP

IT'S TOUGH TO ASK A FRIEND TO LEAVE. THIS IS WHAT I DO: "HEY, MAN, THE RENT'S DUE ON THE 1ST." *~ Big Black*

Once you have decided upon an appropriate "check-out time," you must begin to strive for less-than-excellence in hospitality. Perhaps the toilet paper will go missing. Maybe the heat will turn off. The television? *Dunno—guess it's broken!* As the amenities quickly begin to resemble those of a Rwandan Motel 6, even the most dedicated of freeloading bargain-hunters will decide it's time to start Yelp-ing.

Guy Code conquers all fears. And you must be unafraid to be a terrible hotelier. Remember—when presented with a less-than-glowing review of your service, there is only one reply: *Zagat* the fuck out.

CODE LIST

WAYS TO GET YOUR FRIEND OUTTA YOUR HOUSE

BURN IT DOWN.

BRING IN THE NATIONAL GUARD.

THE OLD "DRUG AND DUMP" AT A BUS STATION.

CATCH A CONTAGIOUS DISEASE LIKE HANTAVIRUS, THAT'S ALWAYS A GOOD ONE.

UNLEASH A LIVE BADGER.

FEDEX HIM SOME ANTHRAX.

CAUSE A CARBON MONOXIDE LEAK.

ASK POLITELY.

CODE BRIEF
DAMIEN'S HORROR STORY

DAMIEN'S HORROR STORY

ATL ✈ NYC

MY HOMEBOY FLEW IN FROM ATLANTA. I HAD TO GO TO WORK AND HE CALLED ME FROM MY PLACE.

DAMIEN'S HORROR STORY

HE SAID "I THINK YOUR TOILET'S BROKEN."

GUY CODE
33

— DAMIEN'S HORROR STORY —

DUMP

HE BROUGHT A DUMP WITH HIM VIA PLANE FROM ATLANTA TO MY SPOT!

— DAMIEN'S HORROR STORY —

WELCOME TO NEW YORK

MEANING HE WAS HOLDING THIS THROUGH BAGGAGE CLAIM...

---- DAMIEN'S HORROR STORY ----

AND THE TAXI OVER.

---- DAMIEN'S HORROR STORY ----

HIS DOO-DOO WAS FESTERING IN MY APARTMENT. THIS IS THE HORROR OF HOSTING PEOPLE SOMETIMES.

THE CODE CONDENSED

▰ DURATION, DURATION, DURATION.

▰ NUMBER TWO'S ARE THE NUMBER ONE PROBLEM.

▰ LEAVE HOTELS TO THE HILTONS.
ALSO THE SEX TAPES AND COCAINE.

CHAPTER 4

CRYING

One time I was, like, watching *Armageddon*,
and I fucking almost started crying.
—VINNY GUADAGNINO

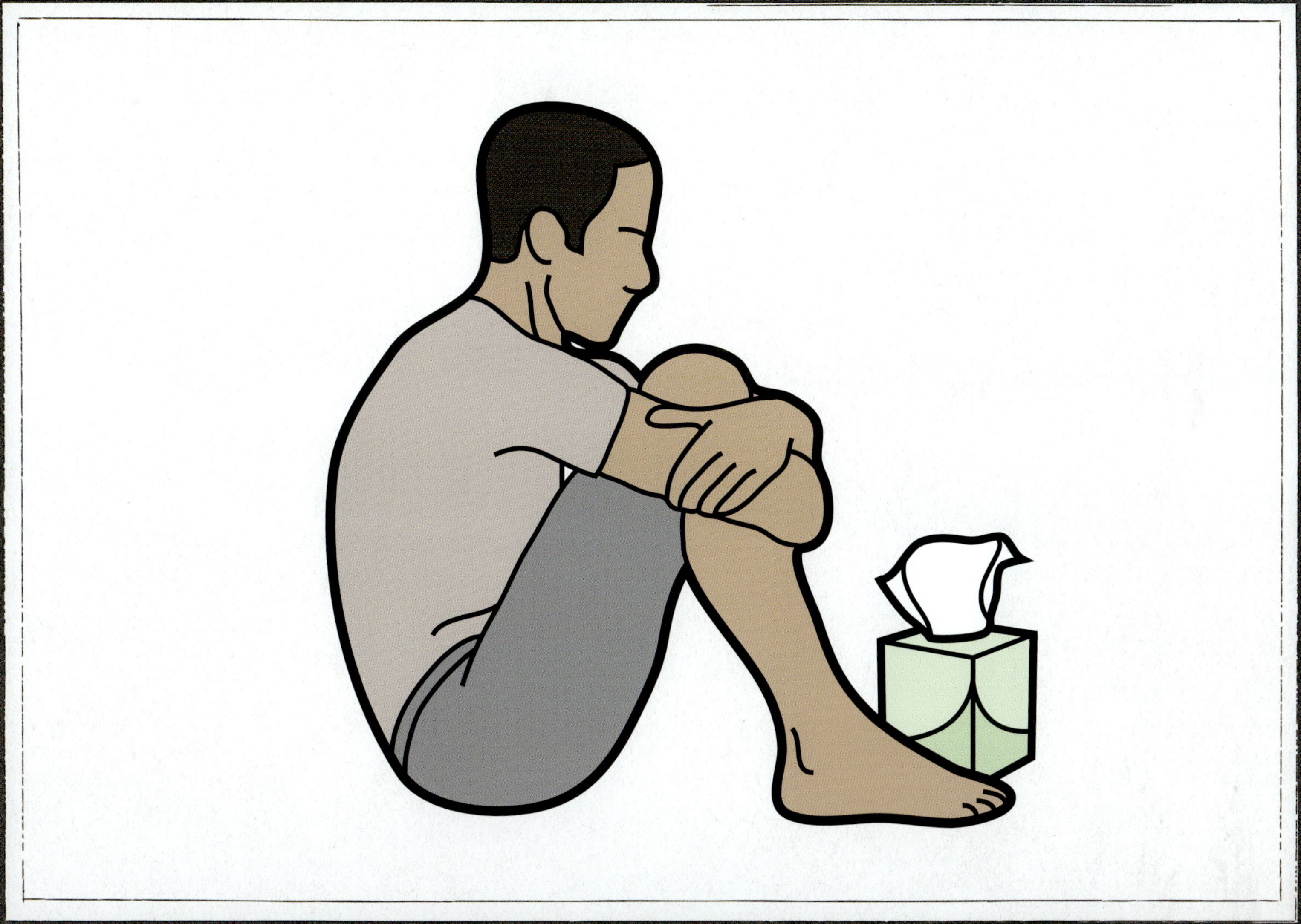

Before I discoverd *The Code*, the question I was most often asked was: "Are you crying?" And though the answer was always different, the truth was always: Yes. Nobody asks someone if they're crying when they aren't. It's pretty rude, when you think about it. It makes me really upset. Now if you'll excuse me, I think I have something in my eye. Don't follow me.

To call me a crybaby would be an insult to babies everywhere. It'd also be pretty inaccurate, since babies can't play Scrabble or Jenga, both of which are highly emotional experiences where it doesn't matter how good you are, because all of your so-called "friends" are big dumb cheaters. I also cried when I lost at *Madden*, twice when my boss yelled at me, and a little bit during *American Idol*. (Phillip Phillips really just *deserved* it, you know?)

Like you, I am imperfect. Learning age-appropriate feelings is a lifelong journey, and the first step is understanding the *Guy Code* to Crying.

I GUARANTEE IF YOU WATCH *THE NOTEBOOK*, YOU WILL CRY.

~ Lil Duval

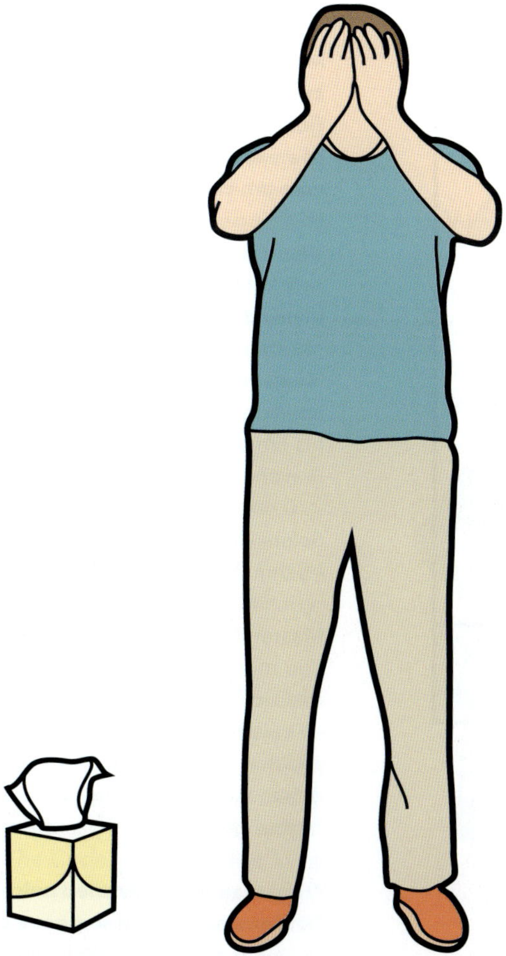

CODE QUIZ

DISCOVER A NEW UNIVERSE OF EMOTION WITHIN YOURSELF (AND QUICKLY STIFLE IT) WITH THIS *CODE QUIZ*:

1 A co-worker just showed you "Best Cry Ever" on YouTube. Did you:

- A LAUGH
- B CRY
- C LAUGH POLITELY, THEN EXCUSE YOURSELF TO CRY

2 Who is your favorite actor from *Two and a Half Men*?

- A CHARLIE SHEEN
- B ASHTON KUTCHER
- C JON CRYER

3 It's 2011 and you're playing for the Miami Heat. Are you:

- A LEBRON JAMES
- B DWYANE WADE
- C CHRIS BOSH

4 While watching *E.T.*, your friend begins to weep. Is he:

- A SENSITIVE
- B COMPASSIONATE
- C MORE OF AN "ACQUAINTANCE"

1 ANSWER

A You cold, cruel, heartless bastard.
B Pussy!
C Okay, I get it. It was pretty moving.

3 ANSWER

A You're a talented but polarizing figure.
B You are unselfish and perform well under pressure.
C You cried and shit.

2 ANSWER

A You're NSFW.
B You're rated G, if you know what I'm saying.
C What? Seriously? That was supposed to be a joke.

4 ANSWER

A I've heard that about him.
B It's true, it's one of his nicest qualities.
C Yeah man, I don't really know that dude either.

ANIMALS YOU'RE NOT ALLOWED TO CRY OVER

COW

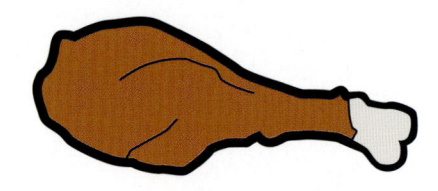

CHICKEN

FISH

HAMSTER

THE CODE CONDENSED

- IF YOU HAVE TO ASK THEY'RE CRYING.

- DUDE, IT'S A VIDEO GAME.

- LEARN YOUR PART, KNOW YOUR ROLE.
  (IF YOU'RE SOBBY DENIRO, AVOID *MEN OF HONOR*).

- CONTROL THE FLOW: THROUGH TEARS ARE A FINE LIQUOR, AVOID "POPPING BOTTLES" INDISCRIMINATELY.

- THE DEATH OF A PET IS OKAY (MAMMALS ONLY).

CHAPTER 5

SOCIAL NETWORKING

It's always important to make a great first impression.
Social networks allow us to make that first impression an awesome lie.
—JULIAN MCCULLOUGH

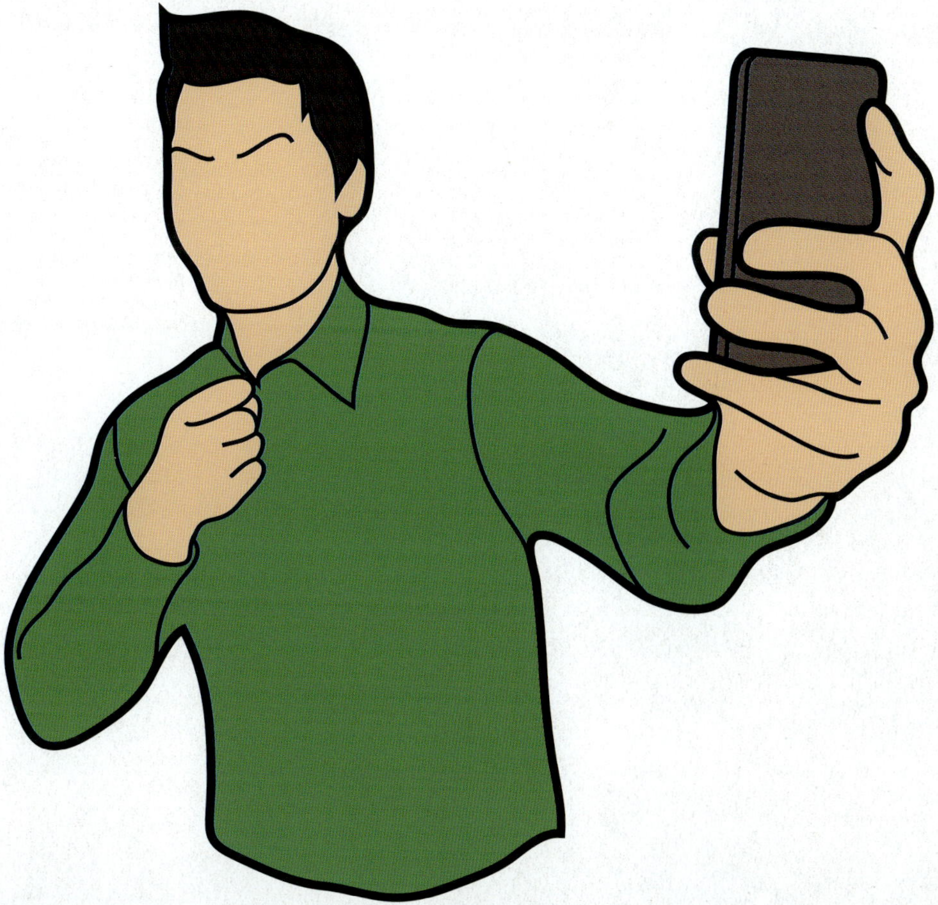

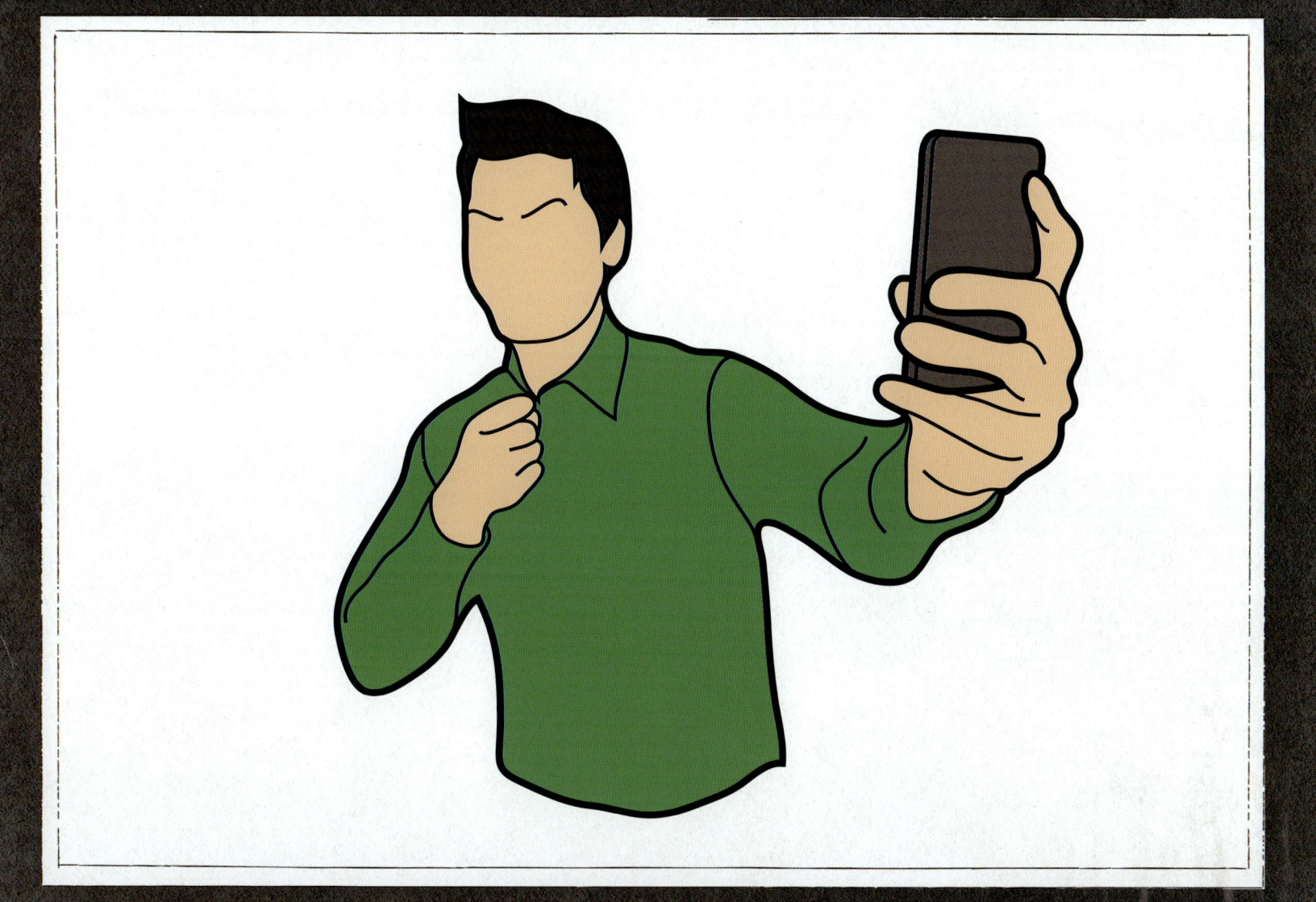

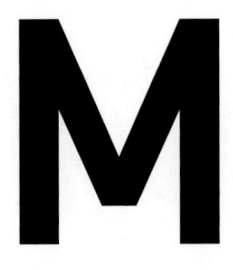

More than simply changing the way we communicate, social networking has actually influenced and altered the trajectory of history. It has provided a voice for the persecuted. It has democratized the dissemination of knowledge. But more important than securing human rights, more important than fighting government corruption, more important even than achieving world peace, social networking has effected perhaps the most profound and celebrated advancement in the way we talk shit and hit on chicks.

With the great power of digital communication comes many difficult decisions—and though I never saw a pair of knockers I didn't "Like," society's sudden overwhelming emphasis on virtual socialization has exacted quite a toll from my already breast-obsessed psyche. Yes—our new, hyper-connected universe is filled with an infinity of splendid galaxies. Unfortunately, all but two of 'em are crazy porn. And those two are actually both Facebook.

Thus, I signed up, as many do, "just to check it out." Also, I heard it's a felony now if you don't. But as my laptop and smartphone became inundated with requests, my mind flooded neurotically with questions: *How do I use this? What photo to upload? When's the best time to update?* And, above all, *Why am I a "Tit Guy"*? (I've heard "Ass Men" have more fun.)

This is the problem with social networking! How do we decide how to represent ourselves? What does our profile photo say about us? Who should we connect with? And how much 'I,' *exactly*, is 'TMI'?

And to think—before *Guy Code*, I was once so confused that I believed I had all the answers *myself*.

Rather than considering social networks a complex and nerve-wracking extension of reality, I simply imagined that there were no consequences. I forced myself to believe the *impossible*—that these websites were a utopia of freedom—the ultimate haven of unlimited human expression, free of judgement, brimming with compassion, and ravenous for gratuitous information. Yes—I would be *me* in my most uninhibited form! I would share *everything*. My trip to the urologist? *Tweeted it*. Bagel or bialy? *I'll consult cyberspace!* "Self," I said, late one Friday night: "It is true. Jake Gyllenhaal was alright in *Brokeback*, but he was way hotter—like, objectively or whatever—in *Prince of Persia*." Decision made, I left nobody's wall unwritten. The more I shared, the more ecstatic I became. With every blown nose, tied shoe and satisfactory defecation that I chronicled thoroughly in public, I imagined my friends and followers shouting in unison: *Thank you! Thank you for being you! More! More!*

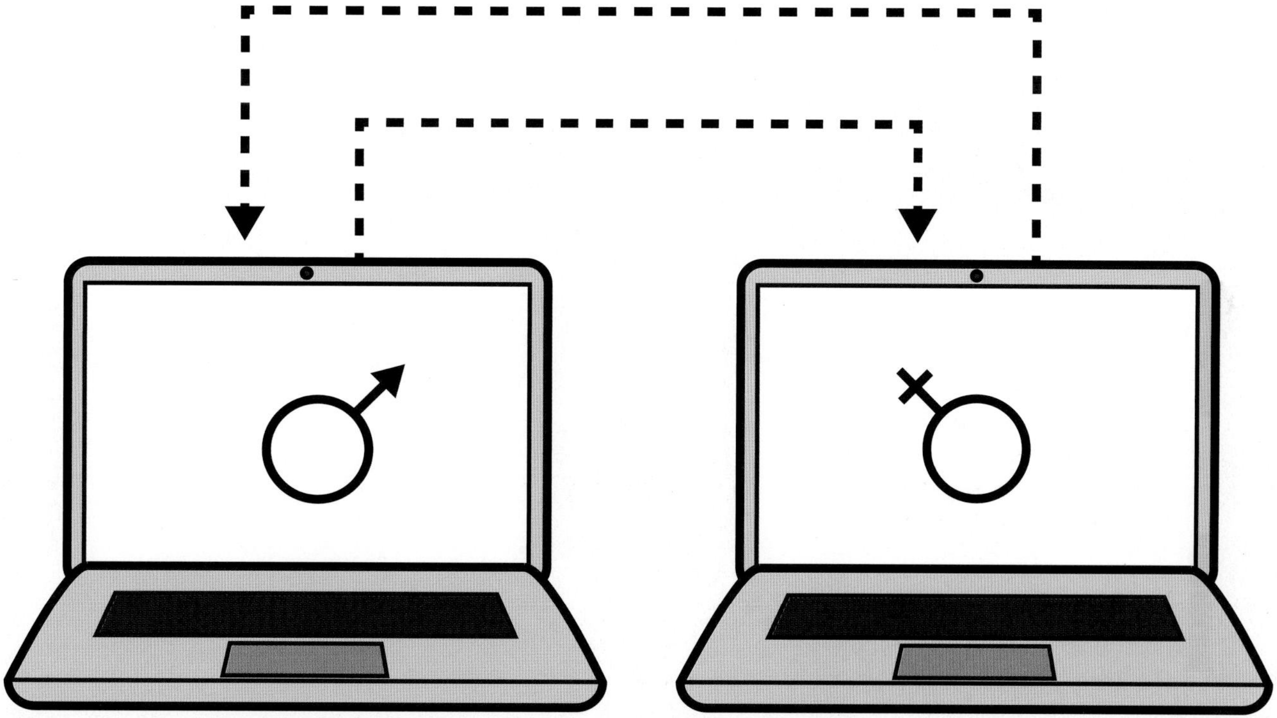

CODE BRIEF
WHAT IF...

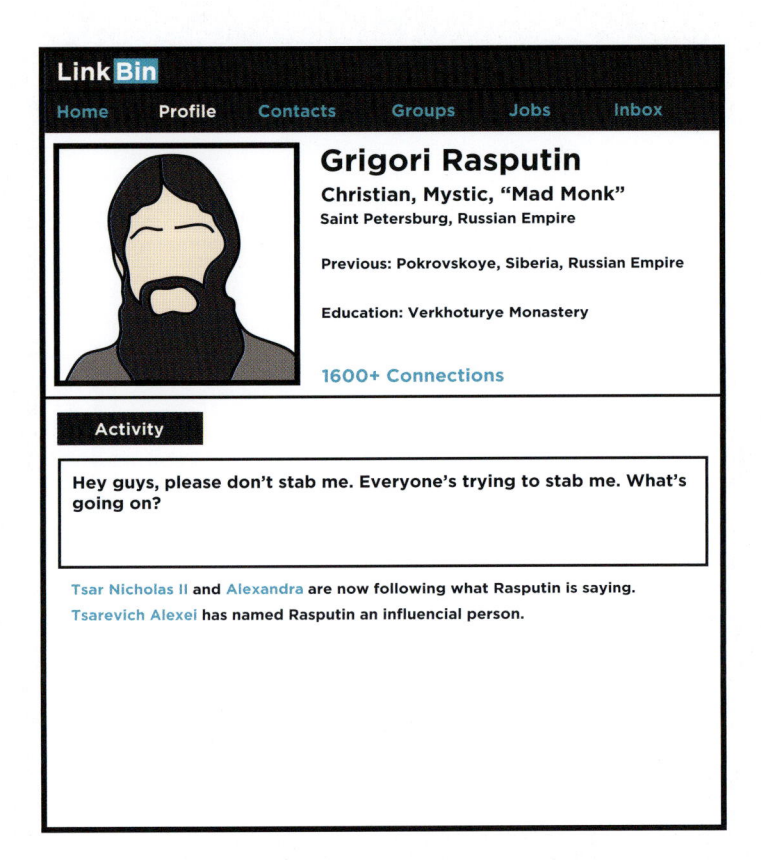

SquareSpot

Adolf Hitler
BERLIN, GERMANY
(mainly)

Hitler just checked into Warsaw, Poland with 18,000 friends!

Hitler is now the mayor of Normandy, France!

Hitler is now the mayor of Belgium!

Link Bin

Home | Profile | Contacts | Groups | Jobs | Inbox

Grigori Rasputin
Christian, Mystic, "Mad Monk"
Saint Petersburg, Russian Empire

Previous: Pokrovskoye, Siberia, Russian Empire

Education: Verkhoturye Monastery

1600+ Connections

Activity

Hey guys, please don't stab me. Everyone's trying to stab me. What's going on?

Tsar Nicholas II and Alexandra are now following what Rasputin is saying.

Tsarevich Alexei has named Rasputin an influential person.

FriendBook

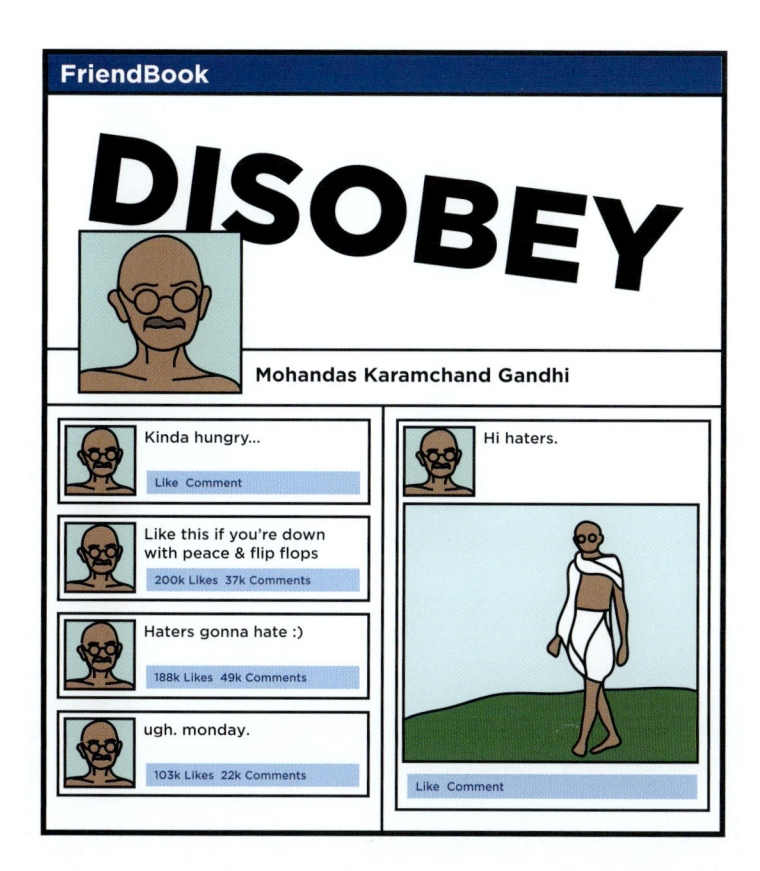

DISOBEY

Mohandas Karamchand Gandhi

Kinda hungry...
Like Comment

Like this if you're down with peace & flip flops
200k Likes 37k Comments

Haters gonna hate :)
188k Likes 49k Comments

ugh. monday.
103k Likes 22k Comments

Hi haters.
Like Comment

Instapix

lincoln_prez65

FORD'S THEATRE

💬 Hope this show doesn't suck!

I would *never* restrain myself. When a negative possibility began to creep in—for instance, that maybe there are some things to be said about another dude's bod that you can't take back—I quickly refocused my energy towards unselfishness, understanding and *Donnie Darko*.

Thing is, it didn't work out so hot. I was paying so much attention to my "majesty of self" that I didn't notice all my friends disappear. I'm not sure what did it, but I think the coup de grace might've been the blow-by-blow analysis of my toenail clippings. However, I was invited to join the Singaporean Jake Gyllenhaal fan club. Not exactly what I was going for, but stuff's pretty lonely now, so whatever. (I'm the treasurer.)

A REAL MAN'S FACEBOOK PAGE SHOULD BE BARE MINIMUM: MAYBE TEN PICTURES, NO THOUGHTS, NO FEELINGS. *~ Julian McCullough*

How did I let things get so out of hand? When it comes to social networking, *Guy Code* has the most followers.

Positivity has power over your profile. Even *virtual* pessimism is a poison. Update your *thinking* before your status—and locate the antidote with these *Mantras of Manhood*:

WRONG: I refuse to keep feelings from the Internet.
RIGHT: *I am delighted to bottle things up inside, mainly because they're humiliating and shameful.*

WRONG: I will never digitally misrepresent myself.
RIGHT: *My regular analog representation needs to keep a shirt on.*

WRONG: I will never Tweet to women I'm unacquainted with.
RIGHT: *Duh. That's what DMs are for.*

WRONG: I refuse to lie about my whereabouts in a status update.
RIGHT: *ON THE G6 HA HA HATERS*

Social networking is in many ways comparable to a job: It is mandatory. It is critical to maintain your professionalism. And it's a great place to stalk your ex-girlfriend.

Besides haunting the online homes of girls past, *The Code* has taught us to harness this powerful technology to encounter girls of the *future*. Yes—we have accepted that Facebook is the world's greatest way to meet women, surpassing even the acquisition of a borrowed baby. But as you prepare to write the glorious pages of a long and storied browser history, you must remember one thing: though everyone has a "type," not everything must be *typed*. When creating an online persona, you must strive always to straddle the *Zuckerberg Line*. Before Facebook: A vindictive nerd with a bad haircut and a dirty hoodie. After Facebook: Pretty much the same, but plus one zillion dollars and really famous. You are somewhere in the middle. Over-sharing the tedious details of your unextraordinary life is a clear violation of *Guy Code's* Terms of Service. However—though crafting a complex and deceptive alter-ego may help you infiltrate the ranks (so to speak), it is also almost certain to hit you with a third act outta *Donnie Brasco*. When in doubt, *leave it out*.

**THERE'S PUBLIC.
THERE'S PERSONAL.
THERE'S PRIVATE.
AND THEN THERE'S TO-THE-GRAVE.**
~ Jordan Carlos

GUY CODE PYRAMID OF DISCRETION

- PUBLIC
- PERSONAL
- PRIVATE
- TO THE GRAVE

IF YOU'RE ON MY FACEBOOK AT TWO AM AND YOU'RE 'LIKE'-ING ONE OF MY PHOTOS, THAT WAS JUST UNNECESSARY.

~ Melanie Iglesias

THE CODE CONDENSED

NKOTB

- SOCIAL NETWORKING IS FOR GIRLS. LIKE, IN A GOOD WAY.

- IT IS NOT A DIARY. IT IS NOT A JOURNAL. IT IS A HIGHLIGHT REEL.

- NO ONE WITH STATUS UPDATES IT.

- NO BRASCO.

CHAPTER 6

BBQs

A. AYODELÉ SANTANA, PH.D., PROFESSOR OF ANTHROPOLOGY:
The grand banquets of ancient Rome were a sight to behold. Men gathered at private residences to recline on lounges, their elbows propped on luxurious pillows. They feasted on fire-roasted meats, fresh fruit and strong fermented spirits. Rousing conversation played an important role, and music was played to entertain the guests. Then they all blew each other. Point is, *Guy Code* was a work-in-progress.

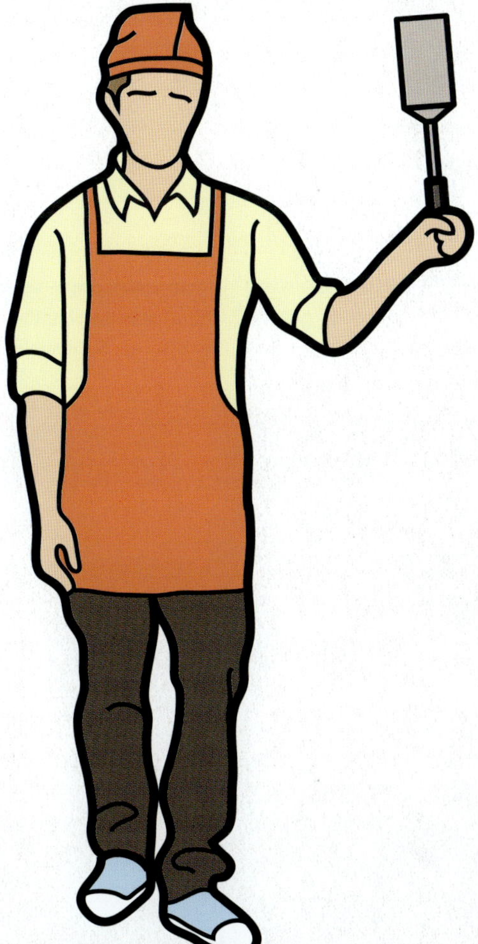

Through the study of archaeology, we know that *The Code* was established long ago. In fact, *Guy Code* is so ancient that it predates historical record-keeping. It predates reading and writing. It predates language! Long before the Romans or the Celts, there were simple cave-dwellers; nomadic, prehistoric men. And in those earliest, most primitive days of mankind, life was short and difficult. Amidst the scarcity and struggle of everyday life, these Cro-Magnons had but three resources available to them: Meat was one. Fire was another. And I think the third might have been ketchup. It was then that *Guy Code* was born.

IF YOU THINK ABOUT IT, THE FIRST PARTY EVER WAS PROBABLY CAVE MEN HAVING A BARBECUE.
~ Julian McCullough

To understand barbecues, we must understand the genesis of *The Code*. We must spiritually re-connect with our birthplace. We must embark on a pilgrimage to the ancient cradle of masculinity. We must travel backwards into antiquity as far as possible, or at least to somewhere before women could vote. Grilling is man's calling. It is our domain.

Though women are welcome, they are not to be in charge. Disregard the sacred lessons of history and you will surely find yourself in a world of doilies, white zinfandel, Josh Groban, and salmonella poisoning.

DR. PHILIP SUTTON, paleontologist:
In accurately recreating the setting of the Upper Paleolithic era, all women at the BBQ should be forbidden from wearing clothes. There's no scientific basis for this, but it's worth a shot.

Most people believe that "BBQ" is shorthand for "barbecue," but the term actually originated as an initialism representing its critical components. The first "B" is for *Beer*. The second "B" is for *Beef*. And the "Q" stands for *Quantity*.

HERE'S THE GAME I PLAY WHEN I'M GRILLING: HOW MANY BEERS CAN I DRINK? *~ Big Black*

Thus, to be successful in grilling, we must assume the roles and responsibilities common at the time of *Guy Code*'s inception. Men were *hunters*. Women were *gatherers*. And gatherers don't mess with the iPod.

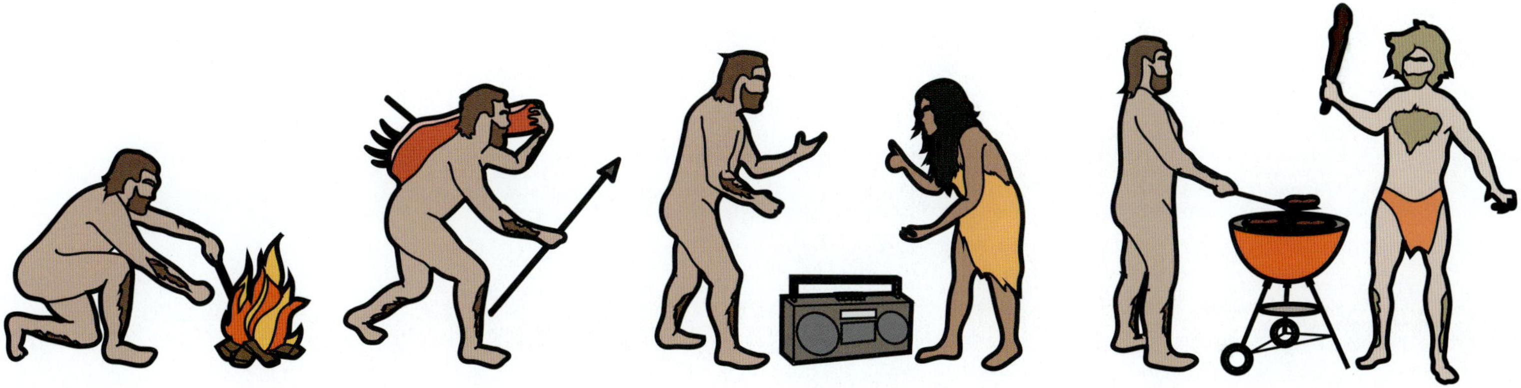

YOU DON'T WANT NOTHING PAST THE '90S PLAYING AT A COOKOUT.

~ Charlamagne Tha God

Over and over again, *The Code* instructs us to streamline our thinking—to distill the essence of maleness, and reconnect with our simplest intuition and instincts. Like many traditions of the Stone Age—such as ore smelting, or R. Kelly's "Bump 'N' Grind"—grilling out is an ancient custom which must be respected and practiced regularly. And, truth be told, you can probably get away with skipping the ore smelting.

A fundamental purpose of barbecues is our convention with nature—to see the sky above our heads and feel the grass beneath our feet—as we nourish ourselves, derive meaning from conversation, and get totally wasted. And just as the great, glorious national parks of America enforce regulations to preserve ecological integrity, a great BBQ also has a list of prohibited items—chief amongst them being hummus. In the great outdoors, the flora is for gazing, and the fauna is for grazing. Also: No forks, knives, cups, or vegetarians.

*VEGETARIAN

CODE LIST

BBQ TRIVIA

The first barbecue was thrown by cave men. The menu included mammoth burgers, pteradactyl wings and Mountain Dew.

The word barbecue comes from the Latin *habeus barbecus*, meaning "fat ass with a spatula."

The Declaration of Independence was written at a barbecue. But no one really started signing it until Ben Franklin and John Hancock showed up with some coke.

From 1923 to 1927 the right to barbecue was prohibited at the federal level, leading to the rampant bootlegging of bocce balls and macaroni salad from Canada.

The longest barbecue in history began in 1692 in Salem, Massachusetts. It lasted until they ran out of stakes.

THE CODE CONDENSED

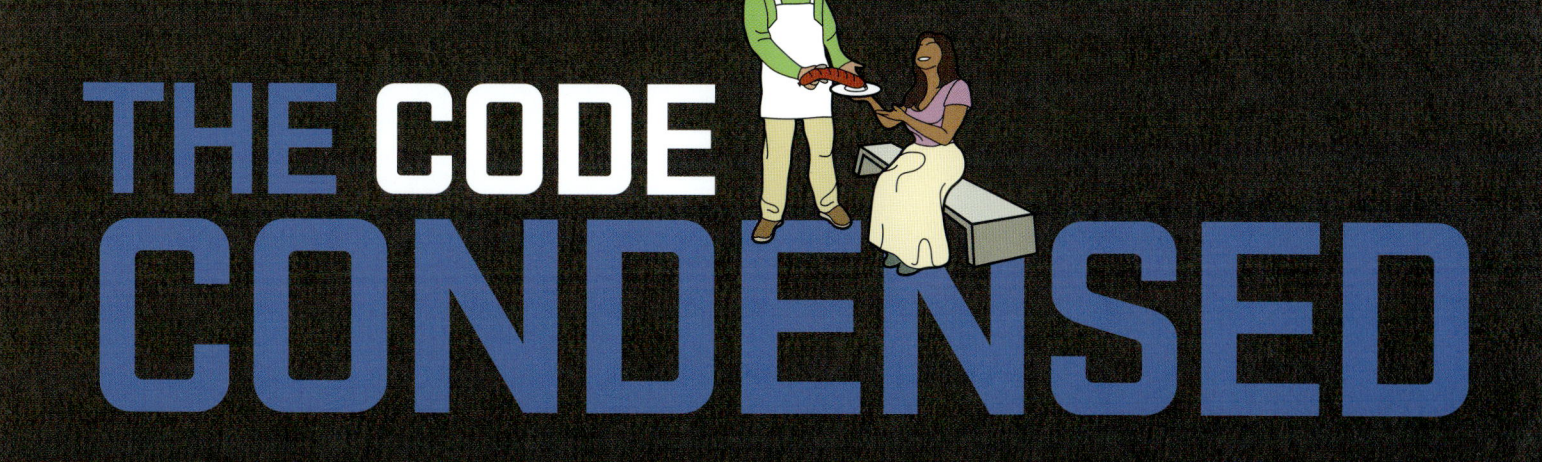

- BARBECUING IS OLDER THAN *GUY CODE*.

- BARBECUING MAY EVEN BE OLDER THAN BOB BARKER.

- THINK DINOSAURS: HERBIVORES ARE LAME. (EXCEPT FOR MAYBE THE STEGOSAURUS.)

- BEER.

- I DON'T SEE NOTHING WRONG WITH A LITTLE BUMP 'N GRIND.

CHAPTER 7

BATHROOM ETIQUETTE

**Rule number one:
Look straight ahead.**
—DONNELL RAWLINGS

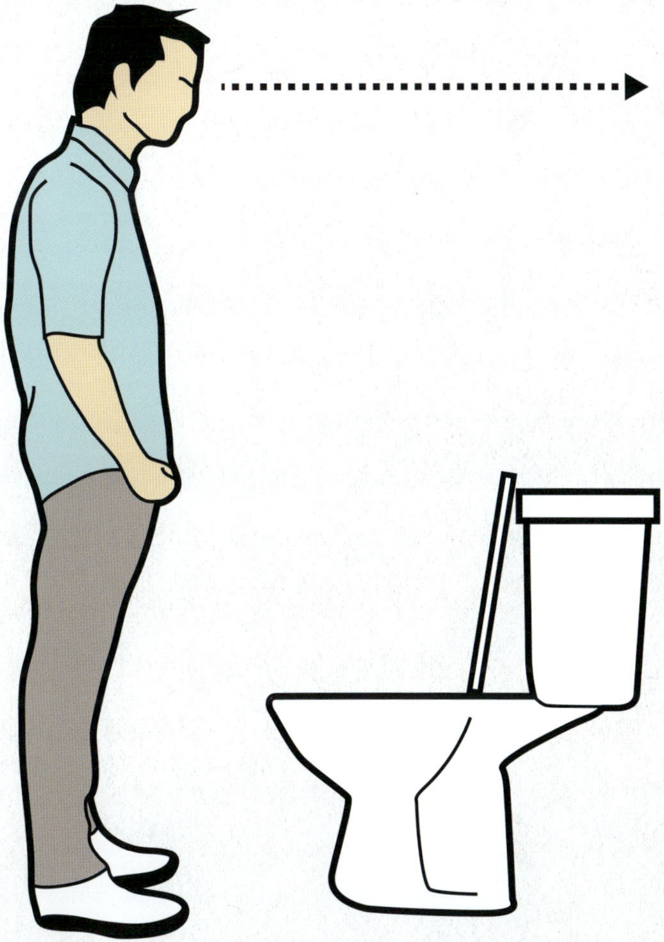

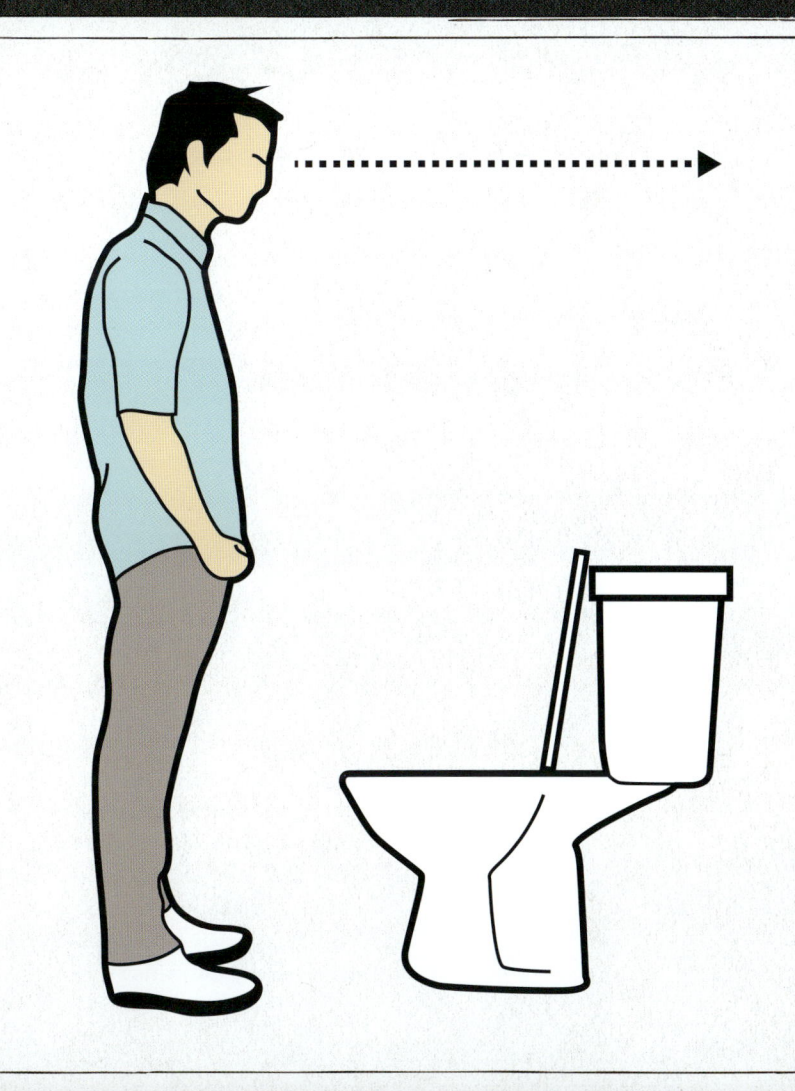

I used to be so afraid of public restrooms that I'd refuse the free soda in any lunch combo. *Better safe than sorry*, I thought. They'd give me double chips instead. My coworkers would ask why I did it, and I'd just smile. It wasn't that I was embarrassed to tell them. It was that my mouth was too dry to speak.

Some consider my fear of the men's room a social phobia, but I disagree. Call me crazy, but I refuse to see anything "social" about excretion. Hey—socializing is okay. Excretion is okay. But *combine* the two and you've got a problem.

The truth is, we've all done things in the bathroom that we should be ashamed of. And I've taken a couple of big ones in public. That's right—I'm talking about *chances*. I've locked eyes with another man at the sink. I've attempted to share space at the hand dryer. (It blows.) I've even attempted conversation with my neighbor in the adjacent stall. What can I say? I like shoes.

RULE NUMBER TWO: LOOK STRAIGHT AHEAD.

~ Donnell Rawlings

Then, suddenly, there was the *Guy Code* to Bathroom Etiquette illuminating everything like the flip of a light switch, and so wisely using a tissue to do so.

To expose your privates in public is a paradox for most non-sex-offenders. Therefore, it's crucial that we handle ourselves with dignity, and handle ourselves not too much. Remember: More than two shakes, and you're masturbating next to another dude.

RULE NUMBER THREE: LOOK STRAIGHT AHEAD.

~ Donnell Rawlings

"Hey, listen: You like what you like, but not everybody needs to know about it. Sure, I love *Gossip Girl*, but thanks to *Guy Code* I've learned not to talk about it to whoever's deucing it in the stall next to me. Apparently, people would prefer to take a dump in peace. Once I learned this principle, everything changed. I won an iPod in a raffle. I found a thesaurus at Subway. So it's obvious that positive thinking creates positive change, which is awesome, but now I know that silence in the bathroom does exactly the same thing."
~ Justin F., iPod owner, Footlong consumer

THE ONLY MAN YOU CAN LOOK AT

Justin's experience reveals a powerful truth: in the bathroom, just about everything is better left unsaid. Though you may have some commanding, frightening, borderline retarded convictions about a television show, a man on the throne best rules his kingdom in quietude. You've entered this place not to move mountains or men, but simply your *bowels*. Do so and leave.

PS: Wash your hands.

PPS: A walk-off grand slam or super sick dunk is probably alright to bring up. But no eye contact.

A public restroom is a complex and dangerous porcelain jungle, filled with many hazards of the mind, spirit, and seat. Just as we must look before we leap, we must look before we sit. You may have heard of the "hover." Men do not hover. We make powerful contact with the bowl. So look first, is all I'm saying. You will not navigate these wilds alone. With *The Code* as your guide, you will experience the life-affirming exhilaration of dropping one at a gas station. But definitely look first.

THERE'S NO WAY I'M TOUCHING ANYTHING IN THAT BATHROOM. I BECOME LIKE A NINJA. ~ *Jordan Carlos*

Just as men must avoid touching any surface in a public restroom so as to avoid exposure to microscopic bacteria, men must avoid positioning too far from the urinal so as to avoid exposing microscopic penises. "Puttin' 'er

SUGGESTED NUMBER OF SHAKES: 1

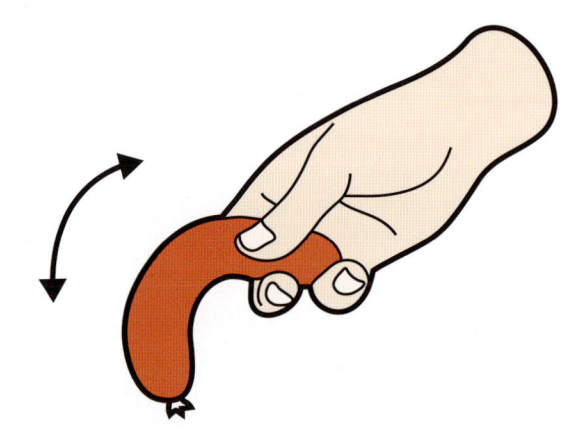

in reverse" at the ol' truck stop is reserved for those with big rigs. Though your Prius may get the job done, it's best if you pull all the way to the gate.

"You know that whole 'One small step for man, one giant leap for mankind' schtick? It applies to the urinal, too. Bring it in a little bit."
—Schmeil Schmarmstrong

Wipe away all anxieties, flush down your fears, and wash off any remaining particles of doubt. This is all that's required for success and good fortune in the john. But also remember to pull up your pants.

ZIP IT

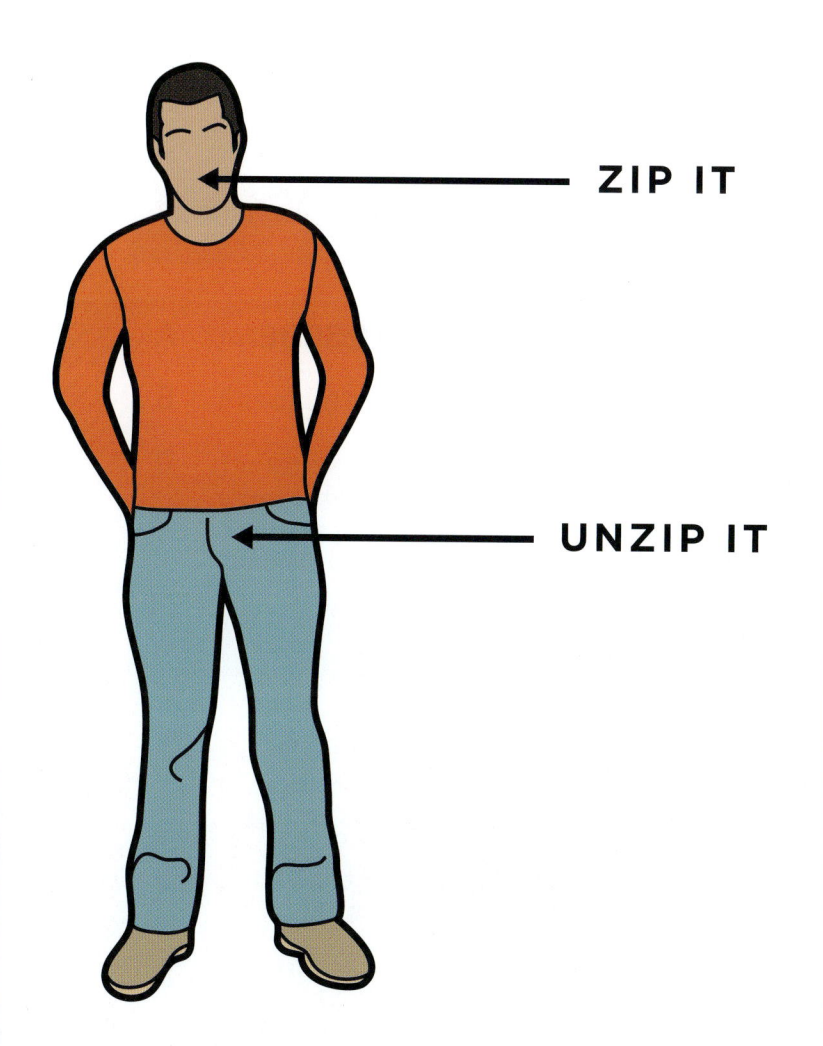

UNZIP IT

CODE CHART

WHAT MEN THINK ABOUT IN PUBLIC RESTROOMS

ONE HUNDRED MEN WERE ASKED WHAT THEY THINK ABOUT WHILE AVOIDING EYE CONTACT IN A PUBLIC BATHROOM:

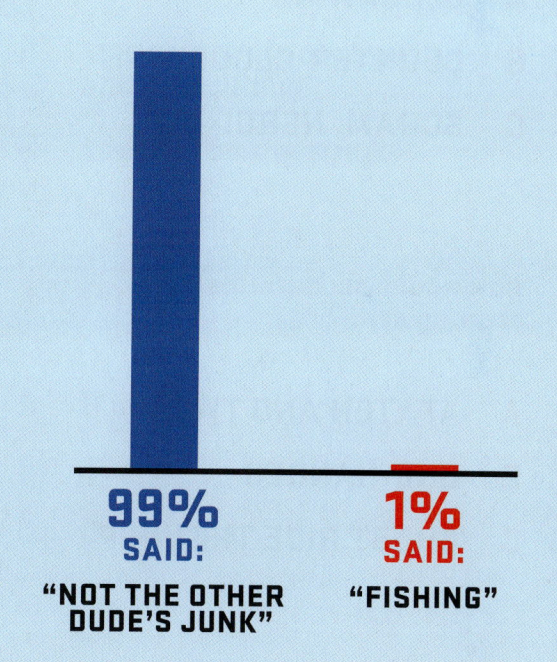

99% SAID: "NOT THE OTHER DUDE'S JUNK"

1% SAID: "FISHING"

Employing the power of *Guy Code*, you will not have to hold it in any longer. And I'm not talking about your "feelings." You will use a public bathroom anywhere, anytime, without fear of inferiority or awkward small talk.

You will know this: The restroom is not the right place for a rest; the bathroom is not the right place for a bath. Move swiftly. Everywhere you look, *The Code* is on your side. But if there are other men in there, use the stall.

RESPECT THE BUFFER ZONE

THE CODE CONDENSED

- LOOK STRAIGHT AHEAD.

- EVERYBODY PEES. NOT EVERYBODY WANTS TO SEE.

- LIKE AN INTERVIEW, GIVE A FIRM SHAKE.

- UNLIKE AN INTERVIEW, DO NOT MAINTAIN EYE CONTACT.

CHAPTER 8

CONTRACEPTION

I'm trying to keep my penis handsome.
–DAMIEN LEMON

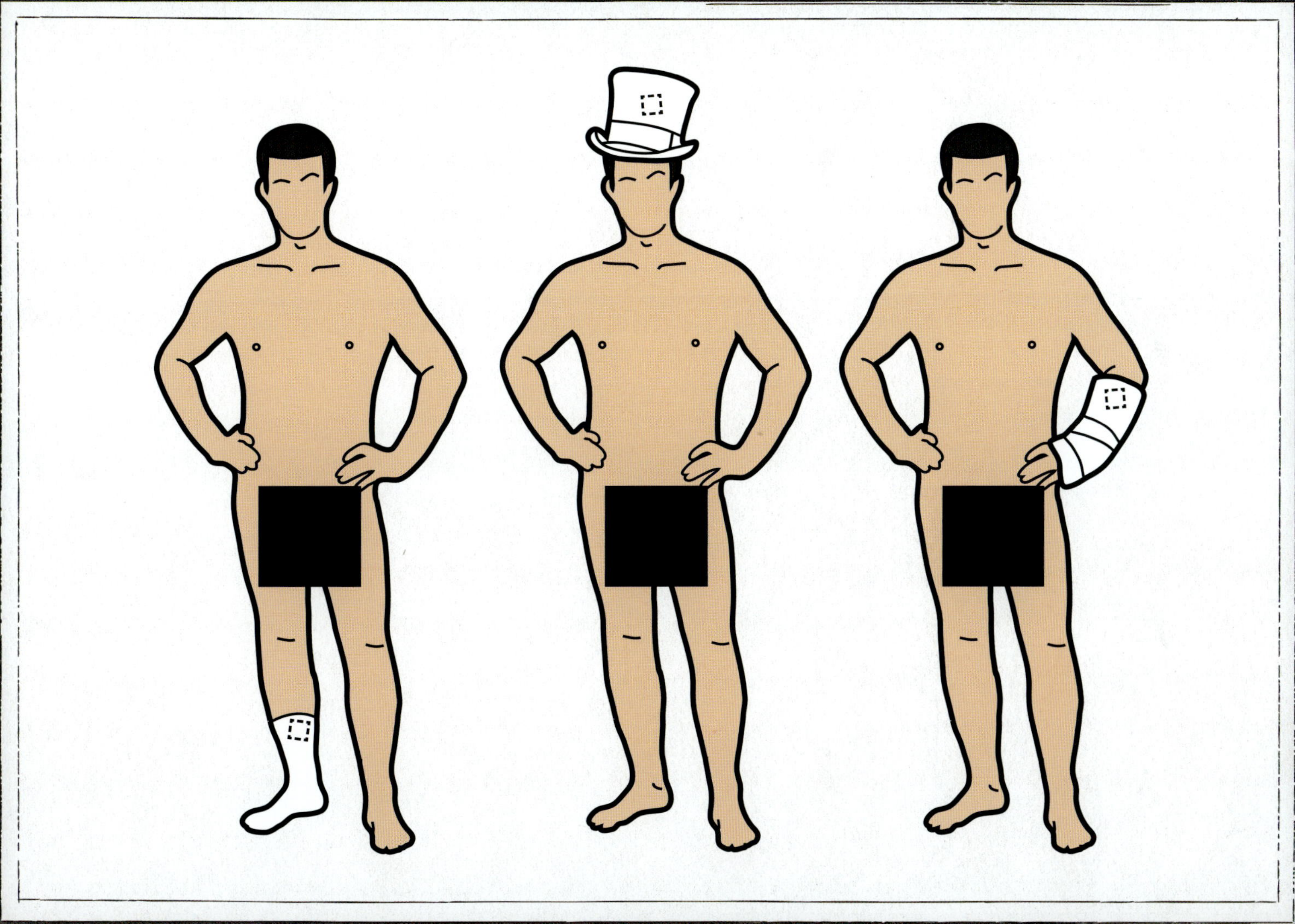

I've never had any reservations about using condoms. Everyone knows what can happen if you don't! And if not *everyone*, then at least Paris Hilton. Hey—though I'd be lying if I said I'd never experimented with drugs, *Valtrex* just isn't something I was interested in trying.

It wasn't *using* condoms that bothered me. *My* problem was *buying* them. Talk about embarrassing! It seemed that no transaction could be sufficiently discreet. Just knowing that the clerk behind the register was tallying not only my prophylactic purchases (amateurishly camouflaged beside a roll of duct tape and a six-pack of Capri Sun)—but also, in all likelihood, the size of my schlong—was too much to bear. And let's face it—condoms come in two sizes: *Magnum XL* and *Everyone Else's Tiny Dick*. You might be able to guess which rack I was shopping.

Well, I lived for a long time without *Guy Code*. And there was a time in my life when I believed I could handle this condom conundrum all by myself—a time without guidance, in which I invented *my own* "prophyl-tactics."

Instead of succumbing to the fear and humiliation of buying contraceptives, I simply forced myself to imagine that every rubber run was *actually* a cause for celebration—a highly anticipated social event, in fact—a commemoration of the penis, in all its wondrous forms!

I'd burst gleefully into the store, practically skipping with excitement. I'd march right up to the first person I encountered, and, without a trace of shame, ask humbly for assistance. "Pardon me, sir!" I'd exclaim with pride, mere inches from his face. "But I'd like to be fitted for a condom!"

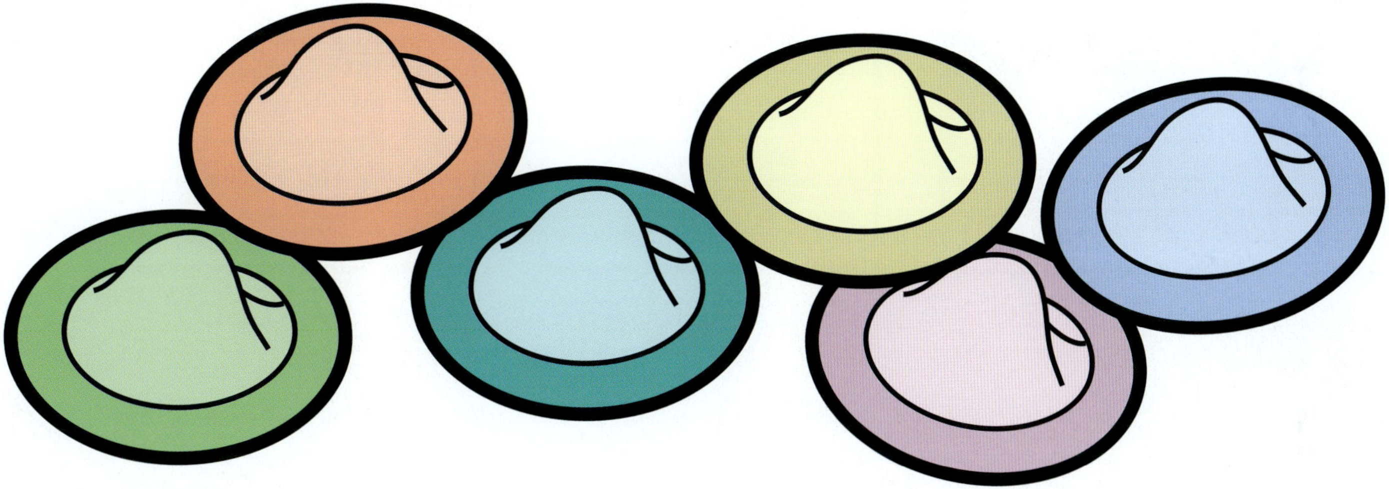

THERE'S ONE FOR EVERY SHAPE

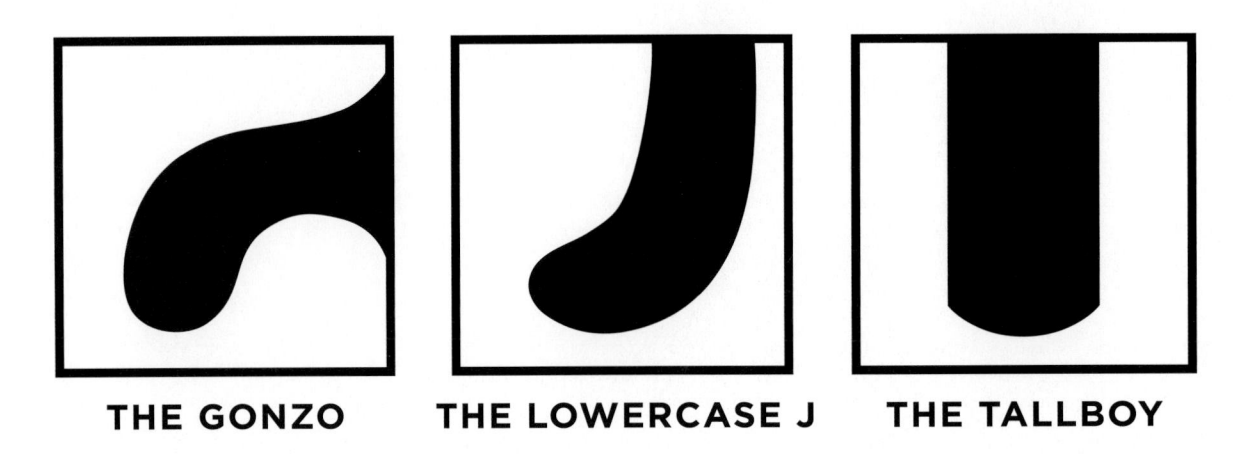

THE GONZO **THE LOWERCASE J** **THE TALLBOY**

To pacify his look of bewilderment, I'd offer a quick elaboration. "You see—my penis is of an *extraordinarily* curious shape."

It was often then that I learned the guy didn't work there. I'd thank him for his time, then move away from the baby foods aisle. But at the checkout line, stacked dozens deep with midday shoppers, I'd begin anew: "Gather round, brothers and sisters! Have you heard the news? I anticipate performing sexual intercourse—*very* shortly!"

The more my emergency contraceptive purchase resembled a televised press conference, the more joyful I became. I imagined a podium and press pool to pivot between—alternately issuing noted proclamations ("My junk hooks left!") and asking hard-hitting questions ("Do you have anything shorter, but *wider*?"). I thought that giving the public an opportunity to weigh-in on what I'd wrap my wiener in was the only way to happiness—and the more intimately I acquainted them with the uniqueness of my crotch, the more praise I'd receive. If a negative and depressing thought crept in—such as, "I think they called the cops"—I'd attempt to immediately remove it, and replace it with the proud, uninhibited one, that was also pretty psyched not to have herpes.

YOU KNOW WHAT'S MORE EMBARRASSING THAN BUYING CONDOMS AT THREE AM FROM A DELI? BUYING HAAGEN-DAZS ICE CREAM AT THREE AM FROM A DELI. *~ Julian McCullough*

Well… it didn't work out exactly how I'd planned. They *did* call the cops. Wanna talk about *embarrassing*? Try getting arrested at Walgreens. Total disaster. You see—though the problem of contraception often seems complex and insurmountable, the only trusted method is *Guy Code*.

Although it's nearly impossible to purchase (or apply) a condom in perfect secrecy, the border between personal discretion and public demonstration is patrolled by our affirmative thoughts. And also, as I found out, the actual police. Thus, rehearse and commit to memory the positive thought patterns found in these *Mantras of Manhood*:

WRONG: Condom shopping should not be an undercover operation.
RIGHT: *I will buy condoms as discreetly as possible, up to and including the application of a high-grade theatrical mustache.*

WRONG: Condoms are treasures suitable for public display!
RIGHT: *I will hide condoms where no one will look: a drawer, a sock, or my autographed copy of Justin Bieber's 'First Step 2 Forever.'*

WRONG: I refuse to use a regular-sized condom.
RIGHT: *Get real, papi.*

WRONG: There's absolutely nothing awkward about putting on a condom!
RIGHT: *Condoms are sometimes awkward. But not as awkward as chlamydia.*

When considering contraception, we must do as the Boy Scouts: discriminate against atheists, women and gays. Or wait—I meant: Be Prepared. Yes—*be prepared!* For though sex may be lurking just around the corner, around the corner from sex may be lurking an infection with the power to disfigure our genitals.

We're all aware of certain three-letter abbreviations that can turn your trunk from Babar to the Elephant Man. New and terrifying STDs seem to invent themselves with each passing day, and the old ones seem pretty ticked off about it. And though we have learned of *The Code*'s incredible power of healing, some of this stuff they haven't invented antibiotics for. Besides—there's simply no telling when we might unwittingly become test subjects for a new and frightening disease, sent from the future to terminate us. The crap that's known to modern science is one thing—but if you're the first guy to come down with MLB, BLT, or the dreaded PS3, *The Code* says you're SOL.

So—wrap it up. Consider condoms as the shoes of sex: without them, there is no service. (But you can probably take your shirt off.)

CODE LIST

DISCONTINUED FORMS OF CONTRACEPTION

THE GUYAPHRAGM

THE INVISIBLE CONDOM

PULLING OUT

IRANCONTRACEPTIVES

SPERMICIDAL JELLO

RENTAL DAMS

POSITIVE THINKING

SPACKLE

THE RHYTHMLESS METHOD

ERECTION, BY CALVIN KLEIN (cologne/birth control)

THE CODE
CONDENSED

- **BUYING CONDOMS CAN BE WEIRD, BUT GOING BLIND FROM SYPHILIS IS TOTES WAY MORE AWKS OMG!**

- **BE REALISTIC ABOUT YOUR SIZE. HE WHO ATTEMPTS THE HINDENBURG OF RUBBERS MAY GO DOWN IN FLAMES.**

- **CONDOMS ARE LIKE EXCUSES: ALWAYS HAVE ONE READY, AND DON'T MAKE IT TOO COMPLICATED.**

CHAPTER 9
FIGHTING

SOLOMON KRINKLE, MILITARY HISTORIAN:
Throughout history, great men have debated the necessity of war. When should we fight?
To preserve freedom and liberty? To come to the aid of oppressed peoples? Or just when someone
calls you 'Chief'? I've studied ancient cultures. I've lived in the forsaken corners of the Earth.
So know one thing about Solomon Krinkle: no one calls me 'Chief' and gets away with it.

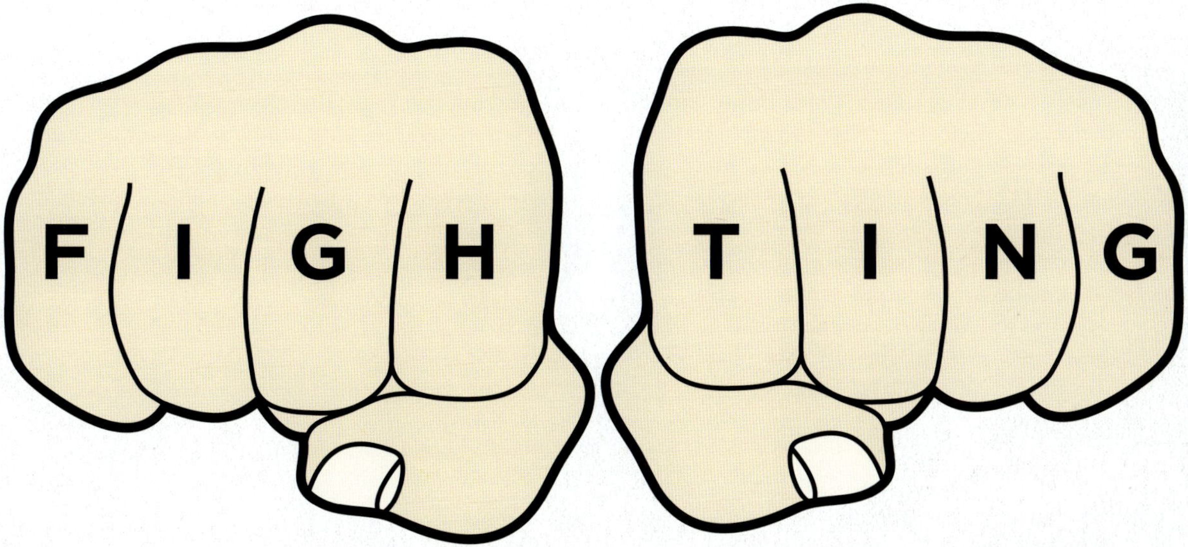
F I G H
T I N G

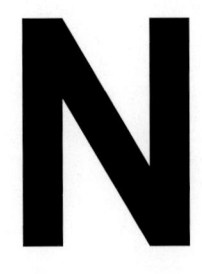

No man wants to fight. Quite the opposite, actually: Man desires *peace*. Man desires *happiness*. But in contrast with these desires is man's urge to assert himself as a human being—up to and including his distaste for a sarcastic nickname. Unfortunately, what with all these *urges* and *desires* floating around, it's only natural for the occasional disagreement to arise. These can escalate very quickly. And though two men may possess conflicting views, we can *all* agree that it sucks to get punched in the face.

Herein lies the challenge central to our experience: when do the gloves come off? When is a disagreement *so* severe and irreconcilable that the only solution is physical combat? When are mere *words* insufficient? And furthermore—once you've done away with words, is it alright to say "OW!"?

Regrettably, no matter one's own peace-loving intentions, few men reach the age of majority without at least a couple *invitations* to violence. And fighting—the prehistoric *Dance of Death*—is an elaborate, elegant soiree, from which many fabulous guests leave limping. It is, in many ways, the ultimate celebration of masculinity.
Thus it begins, classically, with a *Save the Date*:

Dear Sir:

I know you didn't just pull into that spot in front of Yogurtland. I've been sitting here forty-five minutes with my blinker on. Are you kidding me? You've got five seconds. Back it out, or else we're fighting. Invitation to follow!

Until Then,
Your Enemy in the Nissan

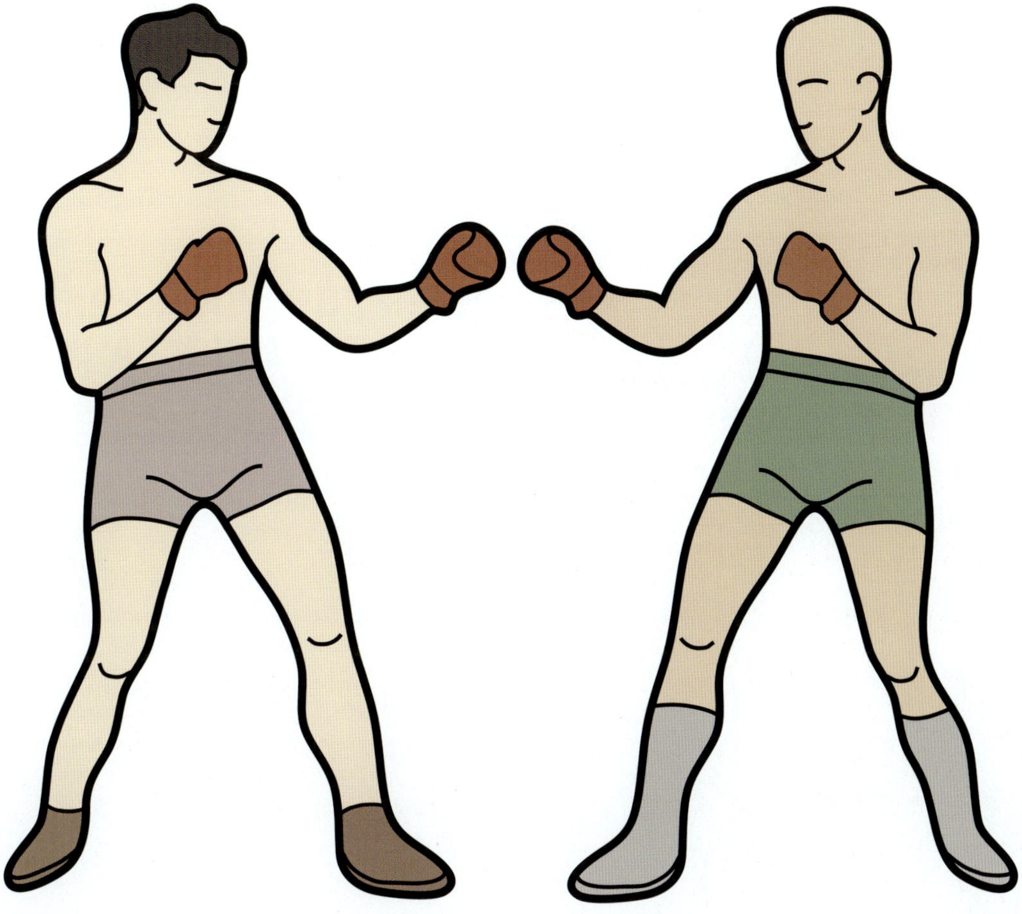

As one has now been politely advised of the event, they may reserve time on their social calendar, make arrangements with their employer, and ask a bro to hold their glasses/cell phone/false tooth. What follows, traditionally, is a *Formal Invitation:*

Hey a-hole:

Me again. Wasn't kidding. That was my meter. I gave you a chance, ya know? So it is now my pleasure to cordially invite you to get pulverized.

Please RSVP:

O   RESPECTFULLY DECLINE

O   WILL BE ATTENDING

O   +1

O   +MY WHOLE CREW

Our prompt attention to this matter is key. But as mature adults, our obligations must often take priority over our desires. And in this case, our obligation is to our face. We must try diligently to preserve its symmetry, no matter how bad we got snaked for that parking spot. Imprudently accepting an invitation to brawl—or, worse yet, imprudently *instigating* a brawl—will lead most certainly to shame, humiliation, reconstructive surgery, and an unplanned cameo on WorldStarHipHop.

YOUR EGO, YOUR PRIDE AND YOUR TESTICLES ARE GONNA MAKE YOU SAY, "YOU KNOW WHAT, I GUESS I GOTTA DO THIS."
~ Damien Lemon

We must not seek the fame of an epic Internet street fight. The popularity of such media is linked directly to the amount of pain and suffering inflicted upon its participants. *Actual death* happens to be a bonus. So although your vid may have received sixty-seven thousand hits, chances are, so did *you*. We must leave bare-knuckled combat to the professionals: Iron Mike. Real Deal Holyfield. And Chris Brown.

That is—unless the *unthinkable* happens.

OPTIMAL PUNCHING AREA

THROW SOME DIRT IN HIS FACE, AND GRAB HIS NUTS. *~ Donnell Rawlings*

The "unthinkable" rarely looks the same twice, but *The Code* will let you know when it's going down. And when it goes down, *The Code* is out the window.

BARON VON ZURICH, Special Advisor to the United Nations:
Land mines, poison gas, weapons of mass destruction, experimental nerve agents and cluster bombs: I have crusaded against all in my mission to limit the cruelty of conflict. But look at my girlfriend once and I won't hesitate to bite your cock in two.

In avoidance of rehabilitative speech therapy, and other consequences common to us "Rocky" types—including wheelchairs, glass eyes, and a peg leg—we must seek the guidance of *Guy Code*. And when there is finally no other option but to fight, we must accept and embrace its solitary rule: *Win*.

To attack a man with fists and feet is an interaction so uncivilized that no laws may govern it. Besides, screaming "NO FAIR" while someone is expertly karate chopping your spine isn't gonna bring your legs back. We have learned from the Internet that those who ask not to be tased are tased immediately. Therefore, we must stay on our guard. We must stay *focused*. And we must stay away from dudes with tasers. If all else fails, do as the Ultimate Warrior: Body slam. Wield a barbed wire baseball bat. And wear a Speedo.

(No one's touching a dude in a Speedo.)

CODE LIST
WAYS TO AVOID A FIGHT

ACT BLIND.

ERR ON THE SIDE OF RUNNING.

DON'T BOGART THE LAST SLICE ALL THE TIME.

DEVELOP AN ALLERGY TO PUNCHES.

START PAYING YOUR CHILD SUPPORT.

MOVE TO FRANCE.

DON'T RIDE THE BUS IN CLEVELAND.

SAY, "NO THANK YOU."

DON'T GO TO DENNY'S AFTER 2 AM.

AT THE FIRST SIGN OF TROUBLE, DANCE SEXY.

THE CODE CONDENSED

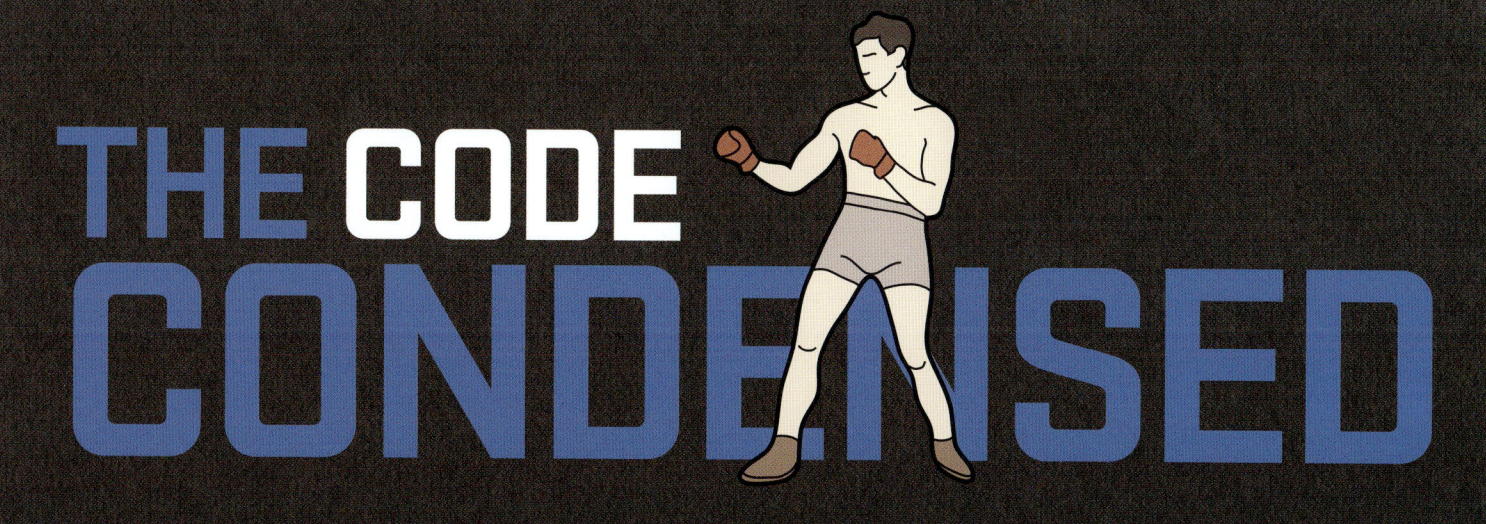

- YOUR FACE IS A VALUABLE INSTRUMENT, AND THE SHOW AIN'T OVER YET. KEEP IT INTACT.

- THE BEST FIGHTS ON THE INTERNET OCCUR BETWEEN OTHER PEOPLE.

- NOTICE HOW THEY NEVER SAY THE LOSER "FOUGHT DIRTY"?

- WELL—DON'T LOSE.

- NOBODY'S GONNA FIGHT A GUY IN HIS UNDERPANTS. (USE THAT HOW YOU MAY.)

CHAPTER 10
SEXTING

We don't want to see your penis.
—DEBRA GOLDSTEIN, AUTHOR OF *FLIRTEXTING*

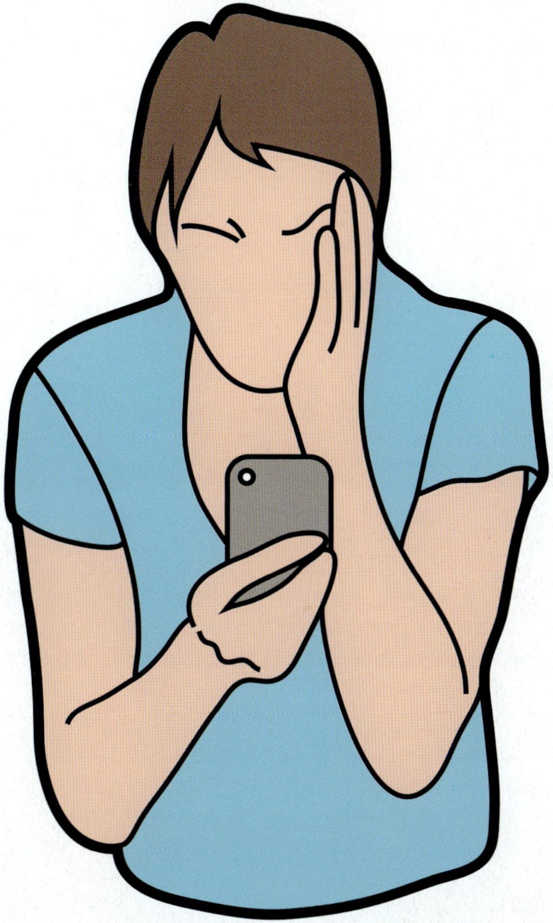

Of all the disturbing things I've found on the Internet, I was most horrified to stumble upon a picture of my penis. How did it get there? Who else had seen it? And, most frighteningly: Only two "Likes"?

I tried to assess the damage. It'd spread virally, which is not exactly the language you wanna use when discussing your schlong. It'd been blogged, re-blogged, tweeted and re-tweeted, remixed and mashed up with some quotes from Mr. T. Yes—I was a fool to be pitied. My member was a meme. I clicked on a link promising nude pics of Scarlet Johansson and wound up looking at my own johnson instead. I'd been dickroll'd.

I panicked. I couldn't leave the house. I was paranoid, anxious, angry, confused, and worst of all, really really hungry. My friends told me to relax. They said that there were plenty of penis pictures on the 'Net—that I was just another pickle in the barrel—an anonymous wang known only to me, my doctor and six girls. Okay, *two* girls.

But there was no disputing who this unit belonged to. As an amateur photographer, I'd made a rookie mistake: I'd included an identifying mark. You could clearly see my appendectomy scar, and the small but awesome tattoo of the Tasmanian Devil. Plus, my face was in it. And also my driver's license. (For scale.) I was an organ donor, and everybody knew. I had given my wiener to the world.

And though I'd tried to deny it, I knew exactly how this had happened.

You see, I'd met a girl at Wawa. I was standing on line for a sandwich. She ordered a tuna on whole wheat. I admired her selection, so I told her so. She was beautiful. We chatted briefly; I asked for her number. She said no, so I just asked the girl making the sandwiches for hers. Same shit.

That night, I agonized over what to say. *Should I ask her to a movie? Tell her I think she's cute? Maybe compliment the sandwich. But it wasn't that great...*

How should I start? What words should I say? Just think! Be brilliant! Be brave! Have confidence, stand out from the crowd...

Yes—I've got it! I'll text her a shot of my junk!

THE INTERNET

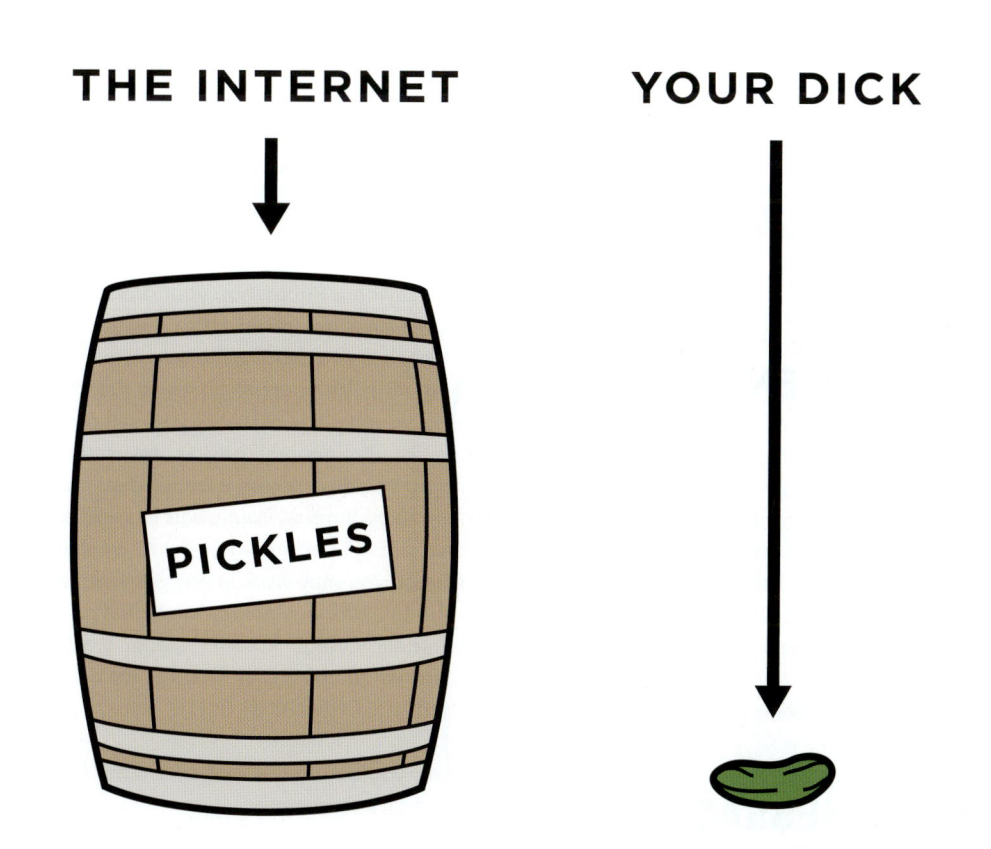

YOUR DICK

PICKLES

CODE QUIZ

EXPOSE YOUR "TRUE SELF" WITH THIS *CODE QUIZ*:

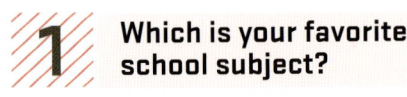

1 Which is your favorite school subject?

- **A** GYM
- **B** LUNCH
- **C** SHOW AND TELL

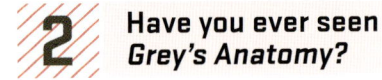

2 Have you ever seen *Grey's Anatomy*?

- **A** NO
- **B** NOT SURE
- **C** YEAH, HE GOT DRUNK AND TEXTED ME A PICTURE OF IT

3 You've been appointed curator of your own "Museum of Romance." Which of the following is *not* prohibited?

- **A** TALKING
- **B** SMOKING
- **C** "FLASH" PHOTOGRAPHY

4 "One man's trash is another man's treasure," but one man's *junk* is:

- **A** DISGUSTING
- **B** REVOLTING
- **C** AND NOT OKAY TO FIND ON MY GIRLFRIEND'S COMPUTER

1 ANSWER

A Just remember: Sports are only important if you wanna get girls and be popular and have friends and succeed at stuff.

B Ask yourself: Are you *really* so proud of your salami?

C You get an A...rrest record!

2 ANSWER

A You didn't miss much.

B Exactly.

C Whoa whoa whoa whoa. What are you talking about?

3 ANSWER

A You possess a relaxed attitude.

B You flaunt convention and popular attutudes.

C You're trying to show the world your cock.

4 ANSWER

A It seems you would prefer not to see another guy's penis.

B Yes, it is apparent you are not interested in strangers' dicks.

C Wish I could say the same for your girlfriend.

YOUR BALLS → "THINKIN BOUT YOU"

SEND ME A PICTURE OF YOUR BALLS? UGH. I DON'T WANT TO SEE THAT. *~ April Rose*

Many men before you have learned their lesson the hard way. Some have even left it *soft*, which is twice as insane. Yes—for those speeding dangerously down the flaccid highway of ruin, the old adage rings true: Objects in mirror are smaller than they appear. But this fate will not await you! With *The Code* as your passenger, you'll know precisely where to make your exit. And no matter what "signals" you *think* you've observed, you will *not* "flash" anyone your "high-beam."

CODE LIST

SEXT CHECKLIST

A CAMERA ✓
A GLAM SQUAD
DISCRETION
A CLOSED SET
WARM SOCKS ✓
IMAX FILM STOCK
A WINNING SMILE
SHAME
FIREWORKS
A JESUS PIECE
DROP CLOTH
4 POUNDS OF RAW LIVER ✓
CRAFT SERVICE
A STUNT DOUBLE
A COCK ✓
A BEAR SKIN RUG
A MUFF
A CAN-DO ATTITUDE ✓
E.V.O.O.
SOMEONE WHO WANTS TO SEE THIS

THE CODE
CONDENSED

[phone: DICK]

- **GIRLS DON'T WANT TO SEE YOUR PENIS.**

- **OR DO THEY?**

- **IN CONCLUSION, THEY MIGHT.**

- **ABSOLUTELY NO IDENTIFYING DETAILS.
  BE READY TO BRAG, BUT BE EXTRA READY TO DENY.**

- **BUT THEY DEFINITELY DON'T WANT TO SEE YOUR BALLS.**

CHAPTER 11
LYING

Why do people lie? Because nobody wants to hear the damn truth.
–DONNELL RAWLINGS

CAR TROUBLE

TRUTH: STRIP CLUB

What is truth? What is fiction? We ask ourselves these questions every day, often while thinking about Bill Clinton. Why did he do it? (Not the *cigar*—I sorta get that.) I mean the *lie*.

Well—even for those of us who've never set foot in the Oval Office, life sure can have a funny way of putting us on the spot. One moment we're minding our own business—and then, without warning, we're suddenly the point-man for a withering barrage of hard-hitting inquiries. *What time is it? Where's my shoe? Did you proposition my sister at the Cheesecake Factory?* Such high-pressure questions demand immediate accountability—and often, the truth is that we *did*, but it seemed like a reasonable way to kill time while waiting for that buzzer-thing to go off.

Unfortunately, truths like these, if not necessarily leading to our impeachment, might very well get us kicked in the nuts. And therein lies the problem: when the facts do not reflect so favorably upon us, is it simply time to lie? What, exactly, is worth lying about? And when it comes to dealing with our pesky accusers—uh, what, exactly, are they *talking* about?

You see—I was once naïve enough to believe that I could handle this dilemma on my own.

Rather than panicking over the complexities of deception, I simply forced myself to believe that the *truth* would set me free—that my friends and loved ones would deeply respect and appreciate my honesty, and our lives would be lived in a glorious harmony of total for-realness.

My best friend returned from the West Coast with a new hairstyle. He asked me what I thought. *The truth is power! Share in your reality!* I told him he looked like Uncle Fester wearing big-ass earmuffs. Another time, my girlfriend demanded to know if I'd checked out a girl at her niece's graduation party. *The actual is factual! Give 'em the realism!* "Check her out?" I asked. "I banged her behind the omelette station!"

The more truths I divulged, the better I felt—and I believed that with each revelation came my ascendancy towards something like sainthood-crossed-with-MVP.

I would not tell even one microscopic lie, because I knew it would ruin all of our happiness. But when a different feeling began to descend upon me—say, that maybe these people were gearing up to kill me—I became very anxious, and regretted immensely even going to investigate the omelettes in the first place.

DID YOU CHEAT?
(COMPLEX ANSWER)

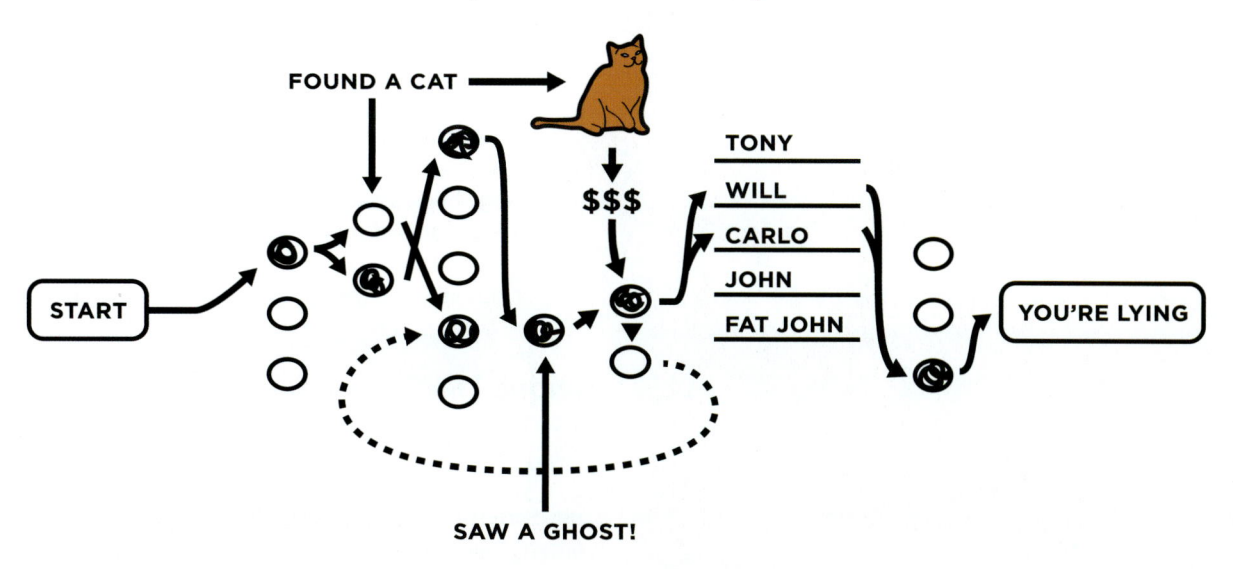

FOUND A CAT

TONY
WILL
CARLO
JOHN
FAT JOHN

START

YOU'RE LYING

SAW A GHOST!

DID YOU CHEAT?
(EASY ANSWER)

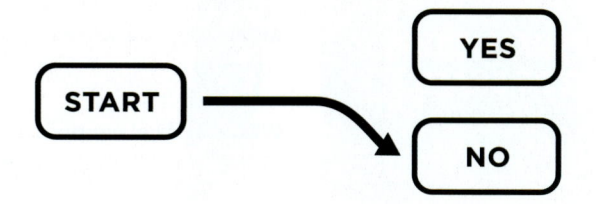

START

YES

NO

I DON'T EVEN CARE IF YOU GOT CAUGHT INSIDE THE VAGINA. YOU SAY: "LOOK, IT'S NOT WHAT IT SEEMS." ~ *Lil Duval*

The difference between truth and fiction is often subjective, but the difference between truth and a brilliant lie is often our job, our girlfriend, a $10,000 fine, and court-ordered community service. To get ahead, use your head.

When it comes to weaseling out of trouble, the *Guy Code* to Lying is simple: *I got no idea what you're talking about*. Despite our desire for a blissful and honest utopia, we are surrounded every day by lies and the liars who tell them—particularly if we're involved with politics or Tiger Woods. It would be wrong to say, "If you can't beat 'em, join 'em"—which is why I'm *writing it down* instead. It's essential to regard your own flagrant falsification of the facts as not only morally acceptable, but actually *in everyone's best interest*.

(Yeah—that's the ticket.)

FILL IN THE BLANKS FOR A BULLET-PROOF LIE*

"HI, _____! I'M SO SORRY I'M
       SIGNIFICANT OTHER'S NICKNAME

LATE. MY _____ RAN OVER A
              MODE OF CONVEYANCE

_____ AND I HAD TO MAKE
ADORABLE ANIMAL

SURE IT WOULD LIVE. DON'T

WORRY, IT DID! I NAMED IT

_____. WHAT A DAY!
SIGNIFICANT OTHER'S DEAD RELATIVE

I _____ YOU, _____."
   NICE HUMAN EMOTION   SIGNIFICANT OTHER'S ACTUAL NAME

***ONE TIME USE ONLY**

THE CODE CONDENSED

- EVERYBODY LIES.

- ESPECIALLY YOUR GIRLFRIEND.

- BAD THINGS HAPPEN FOR A REASON: TO PRETEND THEY DIDN'T.

- ALL LIES HAVE A STATUTE OF LIMITATIONS, BUT EXTRACURRICULAR SEXULAR ACTIVITY IS PERMANENTLY CLASSIFIED.

CHAPTER 12

DRINK LIKE A MAN

DR. HANS FILBERT, PROFESSOR OF EUROPEAN HISTORY:
Long before the colonization of America, males of ancient cultures appreciated the camaraderie and conversation of a late-night session at their local tavern. There, masculinity and social order were often determined via feats of drinking—be they for volume, for speed, or for the uncanny ability to intoxicatedly pilot a horse to the ancient 7-11. Indeed, the unconscious lightweight of yore was regarded with much contempt and scorn—and was pretty much always drawn on with an ancient Sharpie.

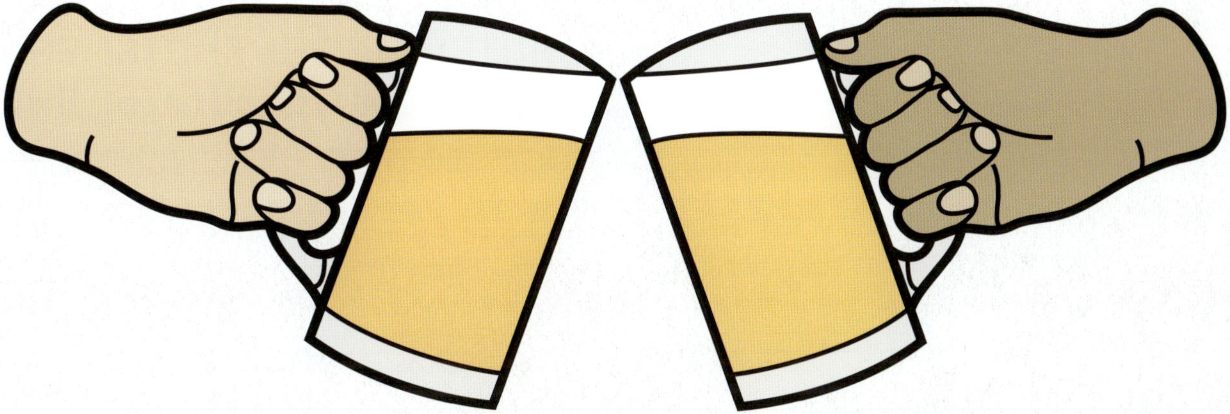

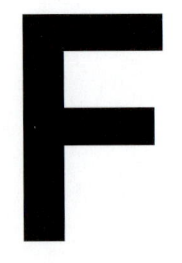

For thousands of years, men have gathered socially to consume alcohol. As far as mind-blowing information goes, the fact that dudes like to drink is no big whoop. Yes—amongst both learned men and laypersons, it is known that the desire to get sloshed with our bros is instinctual. The ingestion of booze is practically *commanded* upon us—if not by some intrinsic, primeval temptation, then usually at least a couple times a year by our married friend who complains he never gets to hang.

Knowing that we will inevitably find ourselves clinking glasses, it is our responsibility to search for the correct methods and and attitudes to apply to the barroom.

The *Guy Code* to Drinking will bring order to the chaos of night. But in the light of morning, it's up to *us* to order a bacon egg and cheese, two Gatorades and a Coke.

WE DON'T MEAN *DRINK LIKE AN ADULT*. WE MEAN *NOT LIKE A WOMAN*. *~ Julian McCullough*

Many marvelous things have come from the mouths of intoxicated men. Vomit is not amongst them. In the absence of bacterial infection or genuine infirmary, the presence of regurgitation is a critical indicator that you blew it. A man doubled over in the bushes is rarely regarded as a sage of wisdom. Similarly indicative is unconsciousness, slurred speech, and trying to bang the fat chick. History has forgotten many of humanity's most hideous atrocities. But have one bad night in St. Louis and you'll never hear the end of it.

SHOTS! SHOTS! SHOTS! SHOTS! SHOTS! SHOTS! SHOTS! SHOTS!
~ Donnell Rawlings

Drinking amongst men is a philosophical paradox: though we must respect our personal threshold for public humiliation, we must also avoid looking like a huge puss. Alcohol giveth— and alcohol *taketh away*. Problem is, you pretty much gotta taketh down whatever you're giveth. Is it a better fate to puke in one's hat than be called a two beer you-know-what? Few know the answer, but I think it depends on the hat.

UMBRELLAS AND PINEAPPLES: IF THERE'S NO SAND AROUND, THEN YOU ARE IN CLEAR VIOLATION.
~ Damien Lemon

HOLD YOUR LIQUOR

NOT LIKE THIS

DR. BERNARD RUDNER, gastroenterologist:
It is a fact of human digestion that sweet and sugary substances help speed the metabolism of alcohol. It's also a fact that fruity drinks are for girls and Perez Hilton. A beach vacation is one thing—but if I catch you in town ordering a passionfruit daiquiri, that'll answer a couple questions real quick.

Like armed combat and the DMV, drinking is a test of mettle—a rite of passage—that can unite men in glorious victory or destroy their spirit entirely. The bar is not a place to discover culinary delights or new taste sensations. It is not a place of coddling and compassion. In some cases it's not even a bar, but actually just your parents' basement. Even then, with only the eyes of your D&D friends to judge you, you must consider *Guy Code*.

Nearly every religion in the world features provisions and guidelines for keeping one's spirit pure. Much as believers must keep those covenants to ensure eternal happiness, believers in *The Code* who seek joy must endeavor to keep their *spirits* pure. Preferably straight out of the bottle. Whisky or a 40 oz. in its natural form can be considered the center of all that is right. But the further one moves away from this—through the addition of fruit punch, sparkling pink lemonade, or diet cranberry ginger ale—the closer one draws to Perez Hilton. Which is a shame, because all of that sounds really delicious. Experiment with pear nectar and you might seek forgiveness. Lapse once with raspberry puree and it'll be a couple of Hail Marys. "Accidentally" drink an entire Malibu Bay Breeze and you might want to see your rabbi. But consume even one sip of a Cocksucking Cowboy and kiss your soul goodbye.

DON'T DRINK ANYTHING WITH "TINI" IN IT

THE CODE CONDENSED

- IT IS CRUCIAL THAT WE DRINK LIKE MEN—IF NOT JUST TO SAVE FACE, THEN TO SAVE DICKS FROM BEING DRAWN ON OUR FACE.

- KEEP MAN'S 11TH COMMANDMENT: DO AS A WOMAN WOULD NOT. UNLESS, YOU KNOW, IT LOOKS REALLY DELICIOUS. (IT PROBABLY IS.)

- CONSIDER THE PRINCIPAL RULE OF SUCCESS IN LIFE: YOUR ESOPHAGUS IS A ONE-WAY STREET.

- SHOTS!

- SHOTS!

- SHOTS!

CHAPTER 13
THE MORNING AFTER

Freud would say if you left something behind, you feel comfortable.
But he is dead. Take all your stuff and get outta there.
—JORDAN CARLOS

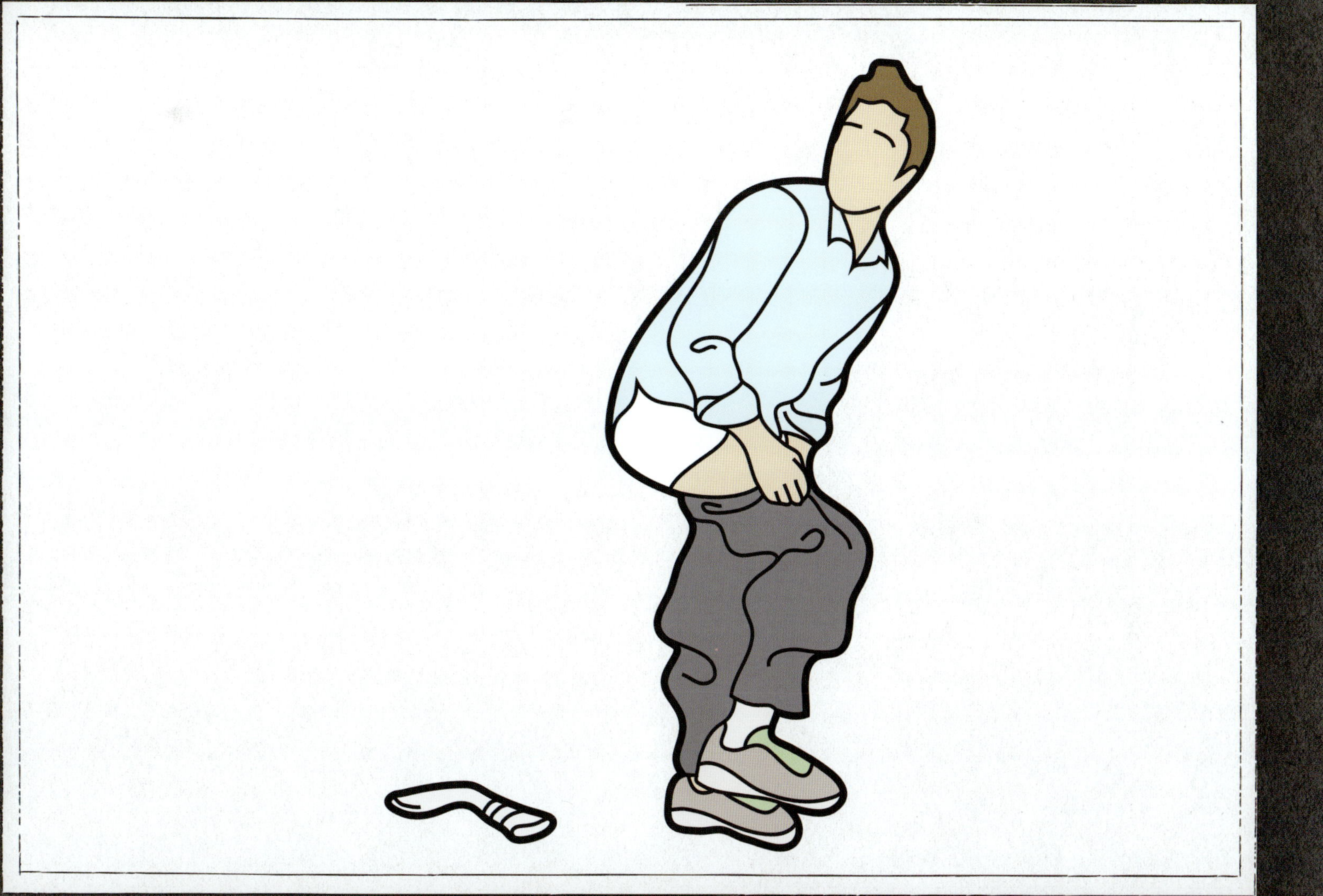

In the best of circumstances, we know when sex will happen. In the worst of circumstances, we're not even sure it's happening while we're having it, and wonder for weeks afterwards what exactly went down. The fact is, when it comes to casual screwing, we're only really *sure* of one thing: anonymous sex with a stranger can happen at any time. And, like many of life's surprises, it can be a double-edged sword. On the one hand, there's the sex. On the other hand, there's the horrible stuff that happens *after* the sex: saggy pillows, grotesque snoring, awkward small talk and multigrain cereal. In fact, the "other hand" can be so devastating that many men consider using the "one hand" just to masturbate and call it a night. Eventually, though, you're gonna get tired of that. You will venture beyond the gates of your masturbatorium, into the wilds of *spontaenous intercourse*. You will go home with someone you barely know. You will awake to find yourself in foreign territory, delirious and confused—immediately compromised, and in a terribly awkward situation. And when heading into that great unknown, this may be the only piece of information that can save you: *be ready to make a clean getaway*.

No mistakes. No hold-ups. You were "in"—*now you're out*. And without a trace! Friend, you must *always* practice safe sex. And I don't mean wear a condom. I mean *check your pockets*.

Take it from *me:* I never leave the house expecting to get laid. But long story short, I ran out one evening for some 2% milk and wound up waking up next to some girl I think I recognized from the laundromat. Now it was morning. I was far from home. My head was pounding. My milk was gone. And all my money was in quarters.

She was asleep. I had to make a move. I slithered slowly out of bed. The floor was covered in dryer sheets. In the corner, I saw my pants. Strangely, they were folded neatly and wrapped in a plastic bag. Silently, I slipped one leg in. Something was wrong. I struggled to get them over my knees. *They had shrunk!* Panicked and confused, I hobbled one-footed, then tripped violently over a box of Cheer—falling painfully to the carpet, which was actually kind of soft and floral smelling. Suddenly, she awoke—and immediately began inquiring about breakfast! Gripped by terror, I screamed—stumbling out the door and onto the street, but quickly composing myself in front of a school bus. It was then that I realized the most dreaded thing known to man: I was missing a sock.

But upon returning to my apartment, I discovered it was not only my sock that'd been misplaced. I was missing my phone, my wallet, my keys, my passport, my lucky pebble, two good pens and a pack of Juicyfruit. I guess it was a wash.

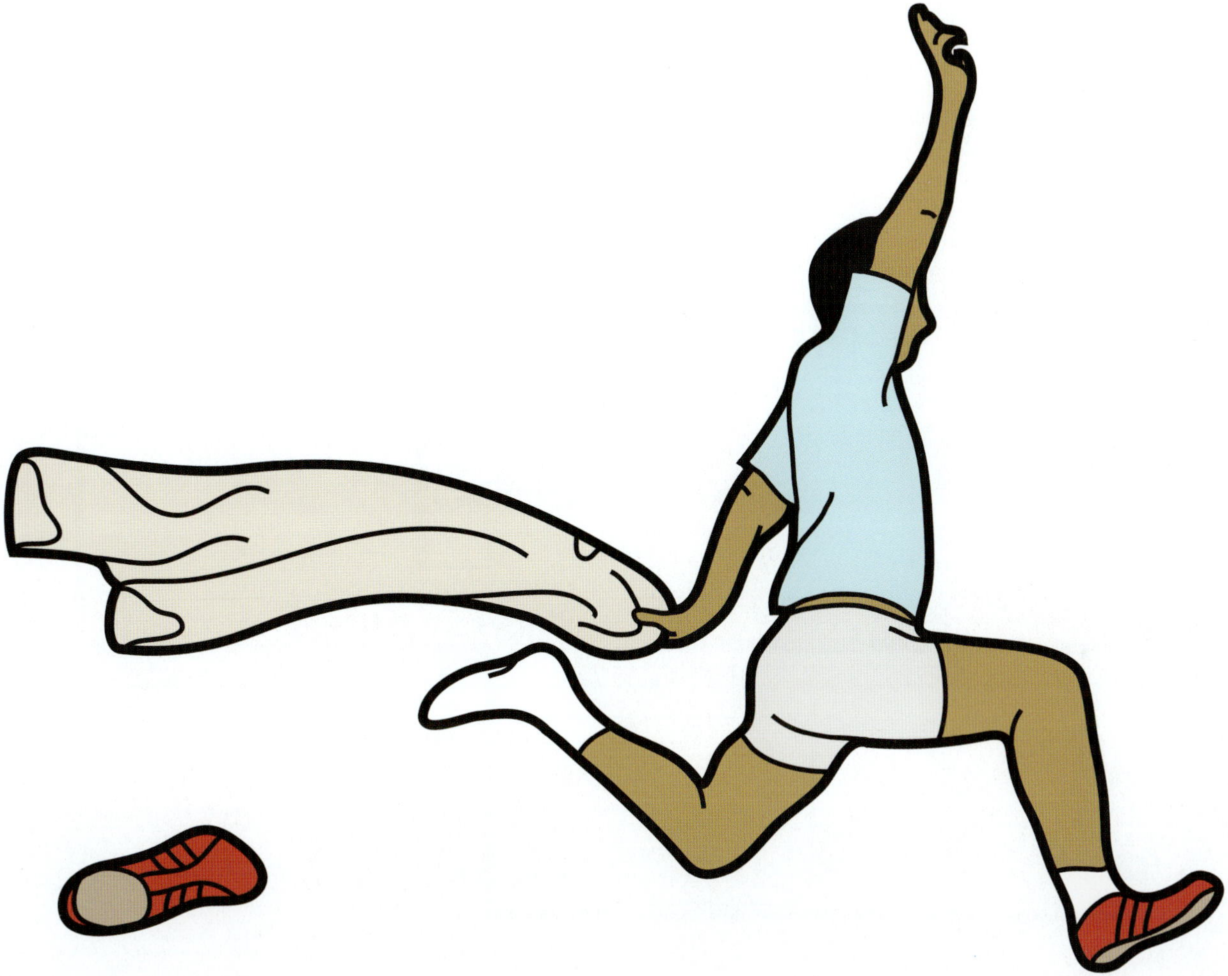

GUY CODE
120

KNOW YOUR ESCAPE ROUTE

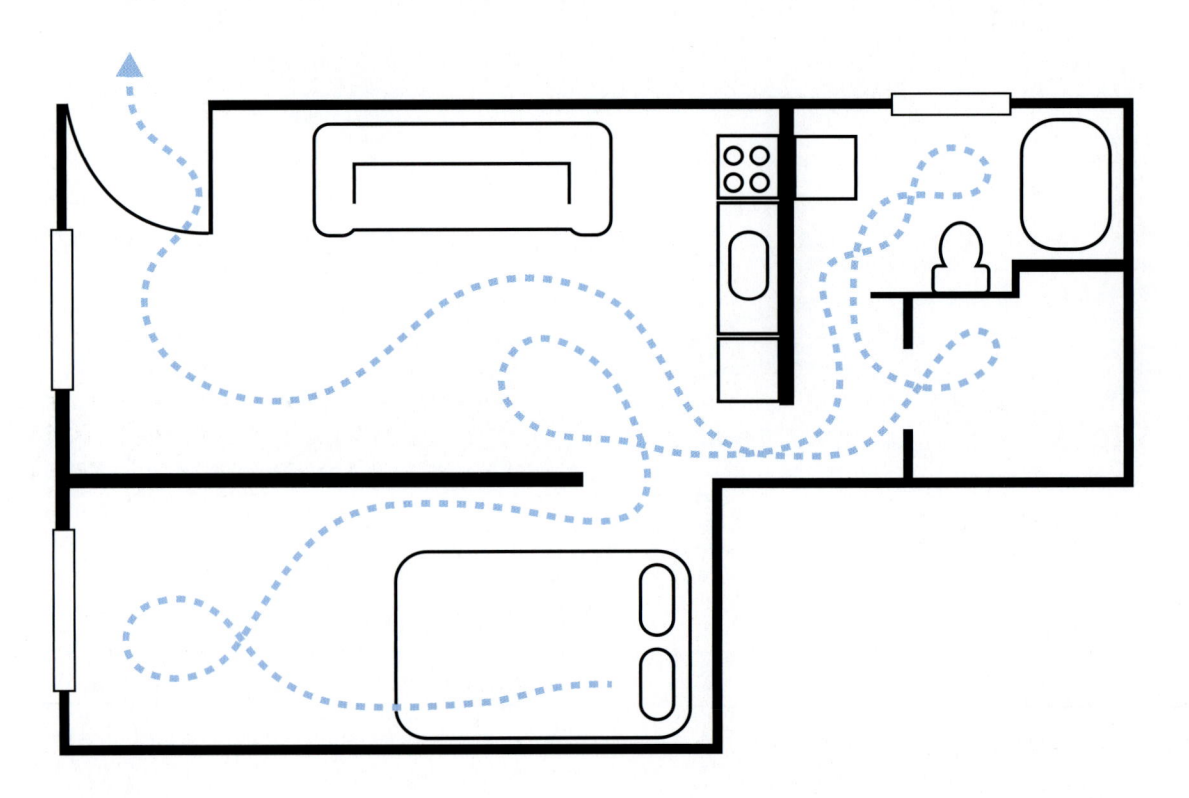

Had I simply known the *Guy Code* to The Morning After, I could've made—shall we say—a more *professional* escape.

CHARGE IT TO THE GAME. COLLATERAL DAMAGE. YOU LEFT YOUR PHONE? GET ANOTHER PHONE. *~ Damien Lemon*

Alcatraz seemed pretty nuts, but a *woman's home* is the most dangerous place on Earth. That it smells nice and actually has a roll of toilet paper in the bathroom is simply the bait—the hourglass upon the black widow spider. Once ensnared in her web, few will escape without looking through at least one photo album.

LISTEN, I GOTTA GO TO A FUNERAL TOMORROW. SO UH, I CAN'T BE FUCKING AROUND WITH BREAKFAST. I GOTTA GET MY MOURN ON.
~ Damien Lemon

However, we are rarely prepared for a woman to enter *our* homes—and therein lies the paradox. When I discovered *Guy Code,* I brought order and cleanliness to the disaster of my life. But my *apartment* is still a rathole. Pizza boxes, porno mags, my electric train set… It's not a good look. I don't need "spiritual enlightenment" to know I can't bring a girl here. If, despite facing certain danger, you have the presence of mind to suggest *her* place, you are beginning to apply the myriad powers of *The Code*. But to begin is not enough. We must be thorough in all our endeavors! We must plan for the road ahead! We must aspire to greatness in all that we do! When we awake in the comfortable, inviting, well-kept home of a woman, we must come up with an airtight excuse for why we gotta get the hell out of there!

"Before I understood *Guy Code*, I was in a very bad place: New Jersey. The only thing I'll say for it is the girls are down for whatever. It's been said that I know what I'm doing in the bedroom. But those people never saw me in the *morning*. I was clueless. *Do you want breakfast?* Yes. *Do you wanna cuddle?* Alright. *Do you wanna walk my dog, run an errand to the drug store, cut my grass, wash my car, and make penne alla vodka for my sorority pot luck?* Sure. What was I thinking? Then I discovered *The Code*. Boom! *Want a glass of OJ?* 'Sorry bitch, my turtle's got pneumonia. Gotta see the vet. Peace!' Now I live in France and I ain't eating brie with no broad. I went from Paramus to Paris!"
~ Tony E., international playboy, former Bergen County resident

From Tony's story we learn that life is truly a blank canvas, and the most visionary of artists work in the medium of *bullshit*. The impossible is made possible when we *believe*—and sometimes also, when they believe! Hey—though it's *impossible* she *believes* this baloney, you're halfway out the door!

"I cannot tell a lie. But I'll fib some if I wake up next to a deuce."
—George Washington

A great poet said it's better to have loved and lost, but he obviously never had to buy a new iPhone. Luckily, such misfortune does not await you. *The Code* is your bedfellow—and as bedfellows go, it's pretty low-maintenance. Though we cannot predict when sex will occur, it will be relatively obvious when it's happened. The naked stranger hogging the blanket is a dead giveaway. But you will not be caught off-guard. You will move swiftly and efficiently. You are a snake crossed with a falcon. (Unfortunately, I think the chick you did it with might be one of those too.) Thus, you will make a calculated and controlled exit. You will have, at the ready, any number of fictional excuses—including your best friend's engagement party, your nephew's bris, and the pressing emergency of descaling your showerhead. You will proceed calmly, taking care to collect the entirety of your possessions. We know that energy given to the world is returned to us tenfold. But this is not the case with the contents of your pockets. You are never coming back here again. That stuff is history.

CODE LIST

WORST PLACES TO HAVE A MORNING AFTER

DULUTH
KABUL
PHIL SPECTOR'S HOUSE
A CAVE
THE SET OF *THE VIEW*
A DITCH
A DUMPSTER
THE BELLY OF A WHALE
THE ZOO
A MORGUE
THE INSIDE OF A CHALK OUTLINE
A BATHTUB FULL OF ICE
THE FRONT PAGE OF THE *NY POST*
GITMO
DOWNTON ABBEY

THE CODE CONDENSED

- IT'S NOT THAT STRANGE TO HAVE SEX WITH A STRANGER.

- BUT IT CAN BE PRETTY STRANGE TO TALK TO THEM AFTERWARDS.

- THINK LIKE A CROOK: PREPARE AN ALIBI, LEAVE NO EVIDENCE, AND VANISH.

- NEVER RETURN TO THE SCENE OF THE CRIME.

CHAPTER 14

THE FRIEND ZONE

Being in the Friend Zone is like being her big stuffed teddy bear.
And if you've noticed, you've never seen a penis on a teddy bear.

—DEAN EDWARDS

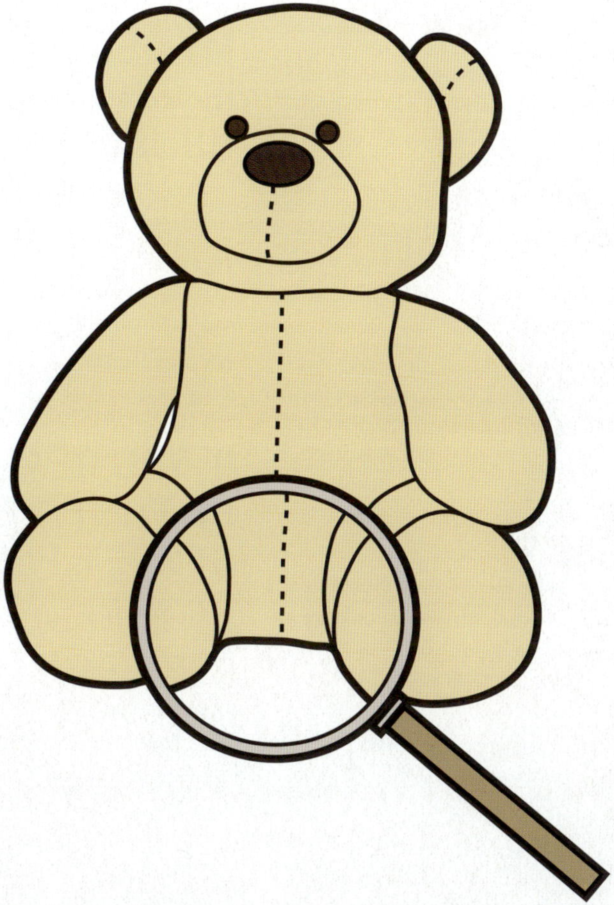

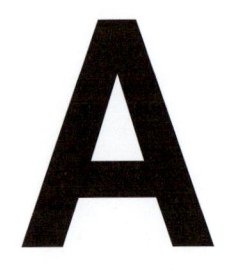

As you continue to recognize the magnitude of *Guy Code*, you will see more clearly certain incredible connections between philosophy and science. Pheromones—an organism's subliminal messaging chemicals—are a powerful, indisputable fact of biology. These chemicals function invisibly and involuntarily, messaging our desires in ways that only our cells can understand. And, though pheromones are beyond our control, what you're unconsciously "putting out there" is the single most important determiner in whether you'll ever "put it *in* there."

But as human beings, we *do* have discrete control of a very unique set of messaging tools: Our behavior. Our words. Our actions. And our breath. A "bad pheromone" day you might recover from. But girls remember bad breath forever.

Dr. Joseph Barone, neurobiologist and sociology expert:
As lower animals select mates on the simple basis of their perceived genetic superiority, so too does the human animal. Pheromones play a decisive role in the sexual selection process. So if you're in the Friend Zone, you got nerd pheromones. Get your pheromones right.

Whereas our invisible chemistry magically teleports us to the Bone Zone, a man in the Friend Zone has undoubtedly communicated an *invisible penis*. Act as though your penis is irrelevant, and you will be treated accordingly. You will find yourself at the Botanical Gardens holding a purse. You will have lengthy conversations about Ryan Gosling and her boss, The Jerk. You will assemble a bookshelf. You will remove an air conditioner. You are a great *pal*—and also, *totally celibate!*

MY DEFINITION OF THE FRIEND ZONE IS: ZERO PERCENT PENETRATION, ONE HUNDRED PERCENT FRUSTRATION.
~ Damien Lemon

Yes—the Friend Zone is a coordinate in the space-time continuum in which a female of the species likes you enough to do stuff together, but not enough to do *it* together. Spiritually, it is a purgatory for erections. Fortunately, there is one surefire way to purify yourself of mortal sin: *whip it out.*

IF YOU REALLY WANT TO GET OUT OF THE FRIEND ZONE? THIS IS A SECRET: PULL YOUR PENIS OUT.
~ Donnell Rawlings

Dr. R. Lee Trisket, clinical psychologist:
There is a psychological phenomenon known as the 'mere-exposure effect.' Human beings tend to develop a liking for things merely because they are familiar with them. Have you ever considered the 'penis-exposure effect'? Think about that for a second.

We've established that success and happiness occur spontaneously for those who tune in to the frequency of *The Code*. But as we scan up and down the dial, we encounter much static, chatter, nonsense and noise—

THE ZONE DESIRABILITY INDEX

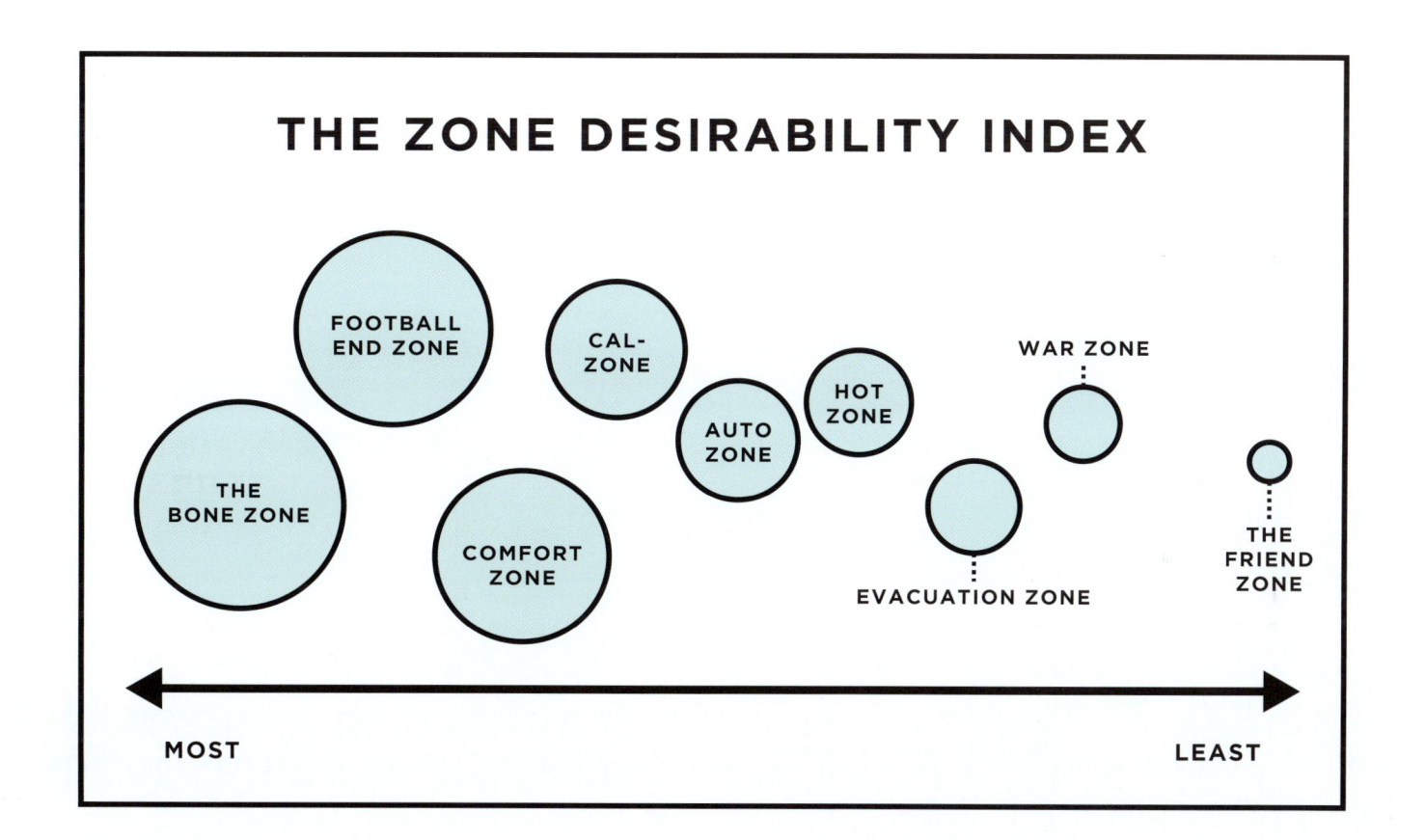

- THE BONE ZONE
- FOOTBALL END ZONE
- CAL-ZONE
- COMFORT ZONE
- AUTO ZONE
- HOT ZONE
- EVACUATION ZONE
- WAR ZONE
- THE FRIEND ZONE

MOST ← → LEAST

including "hair decisions," "office gossip," and "celebrity crushes." Hear any of that crap and you're on the wrong station. From our very first test signal, we must broadcast a message loud and clear: *Quiet please, I'm trying to bang you.* Only by behaving as the savage animal they find most repulsive will you assure their obsessive sexual attraction. Don't ask me to explain it.

It's widely understood that carnivorous animals can sense fear and weakness in their prey. In the wilds of nature, the perception of such inferiority all but guarantees Darwinian selection—a quick and violent death. In human beings, this is known as being a "big pussy," and you're probably just going to the farmer's market, which is actually worse.

DON'T BE A HANDBAG

Perfection is not bestowed upon any of us, and sometimes we discover that we've committed a series of mistakes. The Friend Zone is like a portal to another dimension that opens wider with each misstep. First it's a casual dinner. You pay and end the night with a handshake. Then it's a trip to Macy's. You help pick a sweater as a gift to a "friend." It's a *man's* sweater. Who is this "friend"? She never bought *you* a sweater. Next thing you know, it's "Girls' Night Out." You're drinking a Bellini, mani/pedis all around. The portal has consumed Earth and killed your family. How could this have happened?

The Code shows us that negativity breeds negativity, and also that "Tickled Pink" is not an appropriate color for a man's toenails. But *positive action* can part seas, move mountains, and probably get you a handjob in the fitting room. Thus, the path is illuminated before you: *Make a frigging move! Guy Code* aside—either she's into it (problem solved) or you make things "weird." So? You've got enough "friends." Go get yourself some nail polish remover.

PS: One man's Friend Zone is another man's *Friend of a Friend Zone*. If your platonic activity partner is rolling with some super hot babes, your inter-dimensional portal just got a whole lot more interesting.

JUST GO FOR IT. WHAT DO YOU HAVE TO LOSE? YOU'RE ALREADY IN THE FRIEND ZONE. *~ Vinny Guadagnino*

THE CODE CONDENSED

/// THERE IS NO SEX IN THE FRIEND ZONE.

/// USE YOUR TOOLS OF COMMUNICATION TO CONVEY AN IMPORTANT THOUGHT: YOUR PENIS. ACT LIKE YOU GOT A PENIS.

/// KNOW YOUR EXIT STRATEGY. IF YOU'RE NOT GETTING IT IN, IT'S TIME TO GET OUT.

/// (UNLESS SHE'S NICE AND A REALLY GOOD LISTENER.)

CHAPTER 15

REJECTION

For every girl I've slept with, I've been rejected by ten girls—at least.
That means I've been rejected by like, twenty girls.
—ANDREW SCHULZ

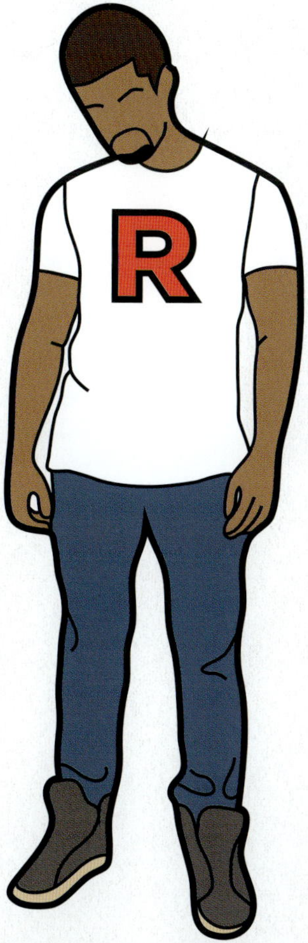
R

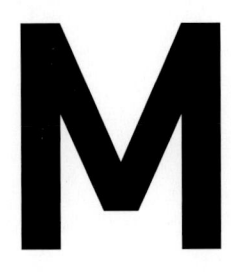

My first interactions with women usually resulted in condescending laughter. Then there was a visibly nauseated disinterest, and a palpable shock, horror, and agitated repulsion. This was invariably followed by my ruthless public humiliation, the complete and total devastation of my ego, and a profound, relentless, cataclysmic depression. Yes—those were the happiest days of my life. It only got worse from there.

I have lived a life of merciless, punishing, torturous, agonizing rejection. It's been said that every man has experienced it. Well, I'm pretty sure I've experienced enough of it for *every man*.

Over and over again, my advances were rebuffed. In the beginning, I'd stew and pace for weeks on end, trying desperately to muster the courage to speak to a girl I had a crush on. I'd visualize the setting, the outfit, the motorcycle helmet I'd bring as a prop. I'd rehearse the scene *thousands* of times in my mind. I'd write a script, then backtrack and rewrite, performing for the mirror and committing every nuance of delivery and inflection to memory. And even then, I might spend another month in my room hugging a pillow and getting really weird before finally approaching her in study hall. There, shaking and stuttering, I'd suddenly come to grips with reality, recognizing that the worst of my fears would never be realized: I couldn't even get the "hello" out of my mouth before her *"no fucking chance."*

Later, girls began to reject me before I'd even decided that I liked them. Surprisingly, they never felt it presumptuous to broach the topic. Theirs was a real old-fashioned attitude: *an ounce of prevention is worth a pound of cure*. Well, I understood what was going on. In this case, the disease was my feelings—and, in a way, their vigilance was something I began to admire. Which is too bad, obviously. Because, you know, their vigilance was making a puke-face.

Soon enough, even girls that I profoundly *disliked* figured out a way to reject me. It doesn't even make sense. Still, I'd wind up back in my room eating Haagen-Dazs and listening to Ani DiFranco. I'd eventually become so fearful of being refused that my life became an excruciating prison, and I lived every day trapped by the bleak, burning, suffering hell of my own mind. Worse than that, you should've seen me try to signal a waitress for a napkin.

Had I known the *Guy Code* to Rejection, I might've treated myself (and my sleeve) with more respect.

CONFIDENCE

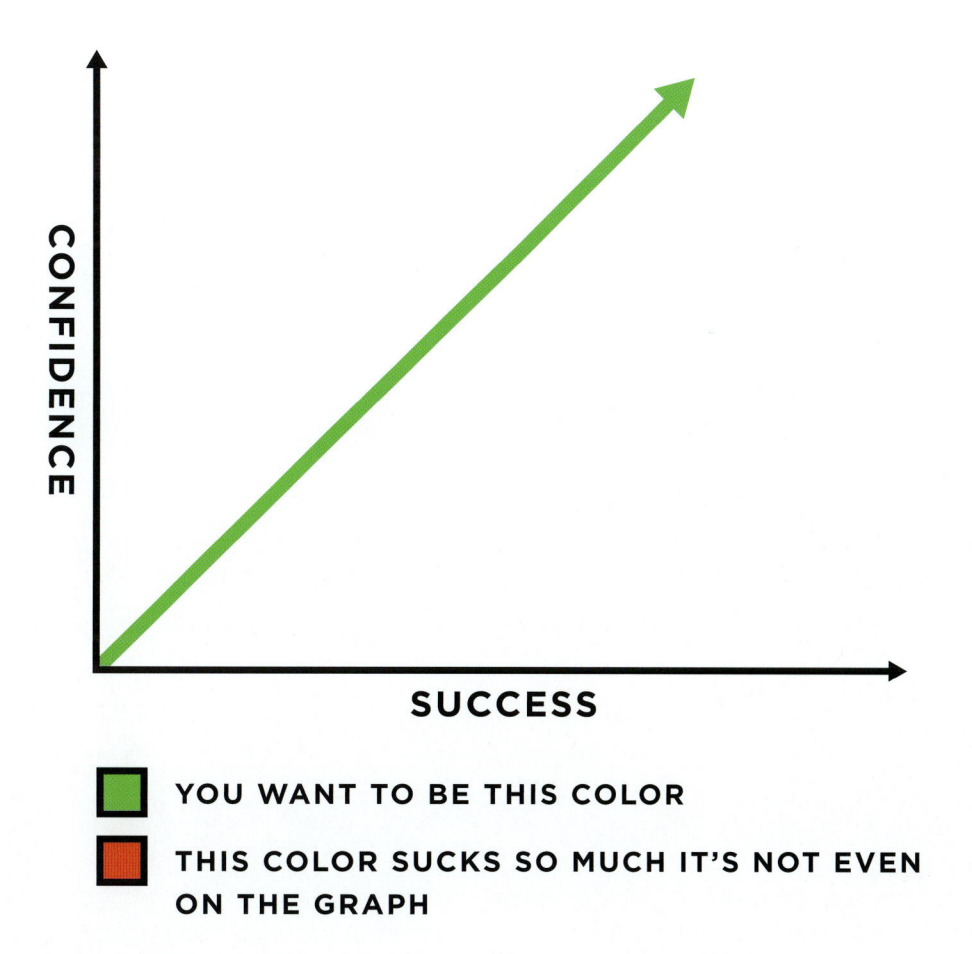

SUCCESS

■ YOU WANT TO BE THIS COLOR

■ THIS COLOR SUCKS SO MUCH IT'S NOT EVEN ON THE GRAPH

HARDEST PARTS OF A MALE	SOFTEST PARTS OF A MALE
TOP OF THE SKULL ELBOWS KNUCKLES KNEES	TESTICLES EGO*

*NEEDS LESS PROTECTION THAN YOU THINK

REJECTION? ASKING THE WRONG GUY. CAN'T RELATE. HEARD IT SUCKS. *~ Julian McCullough*

A man who claims to have never been rejected is either lying, delusional, or Wilt Chamberlain. Life is a series of calculated risks—and though sometimes we find that we've solved the equation, more often than not we discover our math was off. A wise man once said: "Nothing ventured is nothing gained." Another philosophically remarked: "Fortune favors the bold." And a third, perhaps even wiser than the both of them, once asked: "'Sup with that motorcycle helmet?"

It was in that epigram that I first recognized the error of my reaction. Not only is rejection an experience fundamental to one's progress as an individual, I might have fared better with an electric guitar or regulation football.

Thankfully, rejection does not cripple us merely when courting women. No—we are also cruelly denied when pursuing employment, applying to college, trying out for the varsity team, attempting to secure a loan, mortgage, and/or credit card, plus seeking the approval of our family and trying to save a lot of money on our car insurance by switching to Geico.

The list of things I've been rejected for reads like a survey from Family Feud. The topic? "Stuff You Can Have, But Probably Won't." And unfortunately, in my life, the "number one answer" is *"fun."*

"Before Guy Code, girls served me up like I was a contestant on The Apprentice. Never got past the first round. I was the weakest link. They voted my ass off the island. It was devastating. After The Code? Pretty much the same. Maybe worse, actually. They still refuse my invitations. And I don't believe for one second that they 'don't like' frozen yogurt. It's personal, you understand? But the big change has been in my approach. Y'see, instead of approaching their house from the back, under cover of darkness, after scaling the neighbor's fence, I just walk up the front steps and ring the bell. When they don't answer, I get the message—and I find that it makes things less awkward at the office in the morning. And the proof is in the pudding: I just landed the epic promotion, and these new interns haven't met me yet."
~ Jonathan L., Senior Vice President of Sales, still totally blowing it

What is there to be learned from Jonathan's story? For starters, that a lot of crimes go unreported. But secondly, that it is foolish to attempt to prevent rejection. Sure, you can try. But it will reject you.

Though we acquire more experience and wisdom with each passing year, we are never immune from bad timing or bad luck. Some things aren't meant to be. No matter your age, no matter your talents, no mat-

> **I WAS OFTEN REJECTED BY GIRLS BECAUSE I WOULD ASK THEM IF I COULD KISS THEM, WHICH IS WHAT ALIENS DO.**
> *~ Jordon Carlos*

ter your wealth or education—every now and then—someone's gonna tell you to buzz off. And it isn't because you're dull! It isn't because you're dumb! It isn't because you're ugly! In actuality, it's all three of those combined, plus your bad breath. But rather than dwelling upon our mistakes, The Code teaches us to discover dignity in our denial. (Still, it couldn't hurt to floss once in a while.)

YOU FEEL CORNY WHEN YOU GET REJECTED. *~ Damien Lemon*

Rejection builds character. It also builds resentment, paranoia, "trust issues," sorrow, fear and cancer. Thus, the key is to cross your fingers and hope for the character. And in the meantime, we must learn to view each misfortune not as a tragic finale—but rather, as the greatest gift *Guy Code* has to offer: *a valuable lesson!* The pain endured is merely the price of an education. And, as is known to anyone who's filled out a FAFSA, you'll be paying for this shit the rest of your life.

Rejection—and its counterpart, *acceptance*—are a numbers game. *The Code* teaches us that we will fail far more often than we will succeed, and the only measure of true victory is *persistence*. Another lesson bestowed upon us is that after the sixth voicemail, *persistence* becomes a felony. Though your frustration may ferment quietly in your heart, distilling itself into a fine spirit of rage—to be poured liberally over everything, while stroking a tangled beard in a remote cabin in the wilds of Maine—save it for the manifesto, pal.

"Had I known The Code, *it might be easier to keep my glasses level."*
—Vincent Van Gogh

No longer will you be terrorized by the everyday challenges of life. Imbued with the courage of *Guy Code*, you will never fear asking a girl on a date. Save your anxiety for something more terrifying—like asking a girl *how her day was*. On the grand stage of existence, *The Code* is your hype man. And as hype men go, it's dressed pretty conservatively. But you have learned that no matter how carefully we select our outfit, we are bound to occasionally receive boos from the crowd. When that happens, hold your head high. Find meaning, purpose, and new resolve. For it is the very torment of rejection that has inspired the most respected works of art, literature and music—including *Guernica*, *Siddhartha* and "Pop That Pussy."

THE CODE CONDENSED

▰ ACCORDING TO SOME PEOPLE, YOU'RE NOTHING SPECIAL.

▰ LOOK ON THE BRIGHT SIDE: THE POTENTIAL FOR DISAPPOINTMENT IS EVERYWHERE, ALL THE TIME. TALK ABOUT ABUNDANCE!

▰ REJECTION IS LIKE A LOUSY GIFT WITH THE TAGS STILL ATTACHED: ACCEPT IT GRACIOUSLY, THEN GIVE IT TO SOMEONE ELSE.

▰ IF REJECTION IS THE HORSE, THEN DEPRESSION IS THE CARRIAGE. AND YOU'RE SITTING IN IT, ALL ALONE. AND YOU SEE SOME OTHER CARRIAGES JUST LIKE YOURS, EXCEPT THOSE ARE FILLED WITH SMILING, HAPPY COUPLES...NO, YOU KNOW WHAT— IT'S PROBABLY BETTER THIS WAY. YOUR CARRIAGE IS FINE. IT'S PROBABLY, LIKE, FASTER, OR SOMETHING.

EPILOGUE

What I've shared with you in the preceding pages are building blocks of knowledge. Combined, they form a structure that reaches to the greatest heights of guyhood. With this information, you can—and will—live the life of your dreams!

But there is one part of *Guy Code* that I've saved for last.

It's the keystone. It's the fastener. Without it, there is no structure. No matter how well you've studied these foundations and principles, your tower of knowledge would crumble to the ground. Without this small, crucial piece, everything you've learned in this book is worthless.

This is the final component of *The Code*: Don't fuck it up!

Today, *Guy Code* is in your hands. The rest is up to you. And your actions must speak louder than my words. No man can drink the drink for you. No man can take the piss for you. No man can shave your nuts for you. Okay, maybe that last one they could, but I think we've covered this.

You are the secret to *Guy Code*. Tomorrow is a new day. And the glorious history of *The Code* remains yours to be written, for every man, for all of eternity.

No pressure, though.

ACKNOWLEDGEMENTS

The author would like to acknowledge the following for their contribution to *Guy Code*, and for their influence and inspiration in the preparation of this book.

JONAS SALK Leveraged his single-handed eradication of the polio virus to start banging the chick who used to blow Pablo Picasso.
CHUCK YEAGER Test pilot.
BOB FOSSE Possibly the first man to orient his "jazz hands" towards women.
SEAL
DOCK ELLIS No-hitter, LSD.
JOE BIDEN Admitted to the bar, 1969. Hasn't left since.
PAUL REUBENS Taught us that sometimes "Pee-Wee's Playhouse" is actually a crowded porno theater.
PRINCE
JIM ABBOTT Amputee who made it big.
RICK ALLEN Ditto.
RONAN TYNAN Double ditto.
STING
ANTHONY WEINER Learned about scrotographs the hard way.
DAVID PETRAEUS Ran the CIA impeccably, but didn't use Gmail that well.
KATO KAELIN Made a career out of... well, you know.
SINBAD
KEVIN FEDERLINE First male backup dancer to be owed child support.
JOHN BOBBITT One word, two pieces: Penis.
STEVE IRWIN Perished doing what he loved: Fucking with ferocious animals.

RYU Hadoken.
KEN Dragon Punch.
GUILE Sonic Boom.
CHARLES BRONSON Mustache Fatality.
JERRY SPRINGER Never mind the TV show, the acting career, his mayorship, etcetera. This man bounced a check to a massage parlor.
SLASH
ROCKY LOCKRIDGE If you're gonna do something, do it well. Even if it's crying.
KODY BROWN The state of Utah attempted to prosecute him for polygamy, but ignored the crime of his haircut.
RICHARD BRANSON Yo man, I heard he smokes, like, a ton of weed.
FABIO
PETER GATIEN Basically the Captain Hook of partying.
CAMERON GILES U mad?
JOHN MONTAGU Played so many marathon poker games that he had to accidentally invent the sandwich.
KRAMER
RAUL CASTRO His older bro was kind of the bigger deal, but he's been cool about it.
DOM PERIGNON First dude to pop a bottle.
GERALDO
PRINCE FIELDER Heir to the throne of first base.
PRINCE ALBERT Same, but for dick piercings.

AUTHOR BIO

Noah Levenson has written comedy on purpose and by accident for television, radio, magazines, the Internet, and now, a book.

He's worked with Rebel Wilson and Matt Lucas, and toured the world with Brandon Flowers of The Killers. In the meantime, he's written and made things for MTV, VH1 Classic, NBC/Universal, Lionsgate, Screen Gems, Michael Gira of Swans, *Nylon Magazine*, *Heeb Magazine*, and the Canadian men's magazine *TORO*, for whom he maintains a "bad advice" column, "Letters to Levenson."

He's been interviewed for the *Ryerson Review of Journalism* (about telling dick jokes for money), and was once called "nicely anonymous" by *The New York Times*. He was born in New York City and still lives there.

CREDITS

WRITER: Noah Levenson
EDITOR: Wenonah Hoye
INSTRUCTO-ART: Patrick Hosmer
LISTS: Anthony Enstice

PRODUCED BY MTV BOOKS

DESIGN: BRM
PRODUCTION: Walter Einenkel
EXECUTIVE PRODUCERS: Jodi Lahaye and Jacob Hoye
THANKS TO: Ryan Ling, Darin Byrne, Paul Ricci and Amy Campbell

Copyright © 2013 Viacom International Inc. All Rights Reserved. MTV2 and all related titles and logos are trademarks of Viacom International Inc.

FIRST PUBLISHED IN THE UNITED STATES OF AMERICA IN 2013 BY:
MTV Books
1515 Broadway
New York, NY 10036

All rights reserved. No part of this publication may be reproduced, stored in a retrieval system, or transmitted in any form or by means, electronic, mechanical, photocopying, or otherwise, without prior consent of the publisher.

FIRST EDITION: July 2013

10 9 8 7 6 5 4 3 2 1

Printed in Singapore.

ISBN: 978 1938765 11 7